MW01033905

History of Thailand

A Captivating Guide to the Thai People and Their History

Contents

Introduction

Although Thailand's first people are said to have hailed from China and Vietnam, much of their culture was technically adapted from India, Cambodia, and China, and they have had great amounts of Western influence. Despite this, Thailand has certainly forged its own rich and unique history, culture, and national identity. The name Thailand in and of itself has a unique origin story and holds quite a lot of meaning. Though the word Thai is adapted from the Tai ethnic group, who originally arrived in Thailand thousands of years ago, they adopted the name "Thai" in 1238 following the population's liberation from oppressive Khmer rule. Thai translates to "free," which means the country's name holds multiple meanings, both the "land of the Thai," as in the people who occupy it, and the "land of the free." Ironically enough, the country was known as Siam for most of history, and the name would only officially change to Thailand when the country was under an authoritarian military dictatorship.

Thailand's history dates back hundreds of thousands of years ago, many millennia before the arrival of the Tais. Although not much is known about the country before the Sukhothai period, which began in 1238, archaeological sites have revealed that Thailand's territory may have been home to one of the world's oldest agrarian societies and potentially the earliest cultivation of rice.

Migrant travelers from the Tai ethnic group began arriving in the territory that now makes up Thailand around a thousand years ago, and until 1238, they remained under the Mon-Khmer Empire's rule. It was in 1238, upon the liberation from their foreign rulers, that the Tais assumed the name "Thais," which would mark the beginning of the formation of Thailand's unique cultural history. Following its liberation from foreign rule, the country would enter into its Sukhothai period, a time that is often referred to as Thailand's golden era, seeing as it marked the creation and introduction of much of Thailand's current culture, including its language and religion.

By the middle of the 14th century, the Sukhothai Kingdom was absorbed by Ayutthaya, a nearby kingdom, and in time, the population would grow, developing their culture and allowing the kingdom to flourish. Although the Sukhothai period is known as Thailand's golden era, the country would become a powerful force during its 400-year Ayutthaya period. The Kingdom of Ayutthaya would finally be overthrown by Burma (modern-day Myanmar), which would continue to threaten Thailand over the next century.

Those who survived the Burmese sacking of Ayutthaya emigrated to Thonburi, rebuilding their kingdom around this city, which became its capital. In 1782, the first member of the Chakri dynasty ascended the throne, and they have reigned as the kings of Thailand in an uninterrupted chain ever since. King Rama I, the first monarch of the Chakri dynasty, would swiftly move the country's capital city from Thonburi to Bangkok, where it remains to this day.

Thailand, or Siam as it was known then, would be led by the kings of the Chakri dynasty in an absolute monarchy until a civilian-led coup d'état in 1932. Following the long-awaited revolution, the country was run briefly by a democratic government. This democratic government would last barely two years before transitioning to a military government and eventually a fully fascist, authoritarian military dictatorship. Between the Thai revolution of 1932 and today, the government has repeatedly shifted between democracy and

authoritarian military governments due to endless coups, rebellions, protests, and revolutions.

Chapter 1 – Prehistory / Early History

From Before Common Era - The Beginning of the 13th Century

Thailand before the Common Era

Although *Homo erectus* fossils have been found scattered throughout Thailand, recent archaeological discoveries have determined Thailand's first permanent inhabitants settled there around 40,000 years ago. Debatably the most significant and informative archaeological site in Thailand, Ban Chiang, was discovered in 1966 completely by accident when the son of a US ambassador, Stephen Young, tripped and fell, prompting him to notice a buried clay pot in the ground. Ban Chiang, located in the northeast Udon Thani Province of Thailand, contains artifacts that date back to 1495 BCE.

Stephen Young may have stumbled onto ceramic pots, but as further excavations were made, penetrating deeper and deeper within the stratigraphic layers at Ban Chiang, more buried artifacts were revealed that shaped what historians know of Thailand's early history. The discoveries at Ban Chiang revealed early inhabitants might have begun cultivating rice just after 1500 BCE. Other archaeological sites in Thailand, such as Non Nok Tha, where rice chaff was found in pottery, proves the country may have had wet rice agriculture back in 3000 BCE. This is significant since it would make Thailand not only the home to Southeast Asia's oldest known agrarian society but also one of the world's oldest farming communities.

In addition to agricultural discoveries, Ban Chiang contained some of the world's earliest known bronze and copper production tools, which revealed that Thailand might have had one of the most advanced metallurgy industries at the time. These metal-focused excavations, conducted mostly by Chester (Chet) Gorman and Pisit Charoenwongsa, found traces of metalwork, including bronze and iron, dating back to 2500 BCE and possibly as early as 3000 BCE. If these discoveries prove to be accurate, Thailand would have predated metallurgy in Southeast Asia by around 1,000 years and potentially had some of the world's first bronze forgers.

Amongst the ceramics and metal forging tools found at the Ban Chiang archaeological site were ancient bodies, which were often buried within or with these crafted objects, indicating that Thailand's first settlers had burials. The buried bodies that were discovered not only raised questions regarding the early settlers' ritualistic burial traditions but also allowed scientists to run tests that would then lead to further important historical discoveries.

Some studies performed on stable isotopes in the teeth of the people buried at Ban Chiang and other archaeological sites around Thailand have led historians to conclude prehistoric Thailand may have had a matrilocal system (in which a married couple lives with or near the wife's parents). This conclusion stems from test results that found women grew up on local food while men seemed to have been foragers, travelers, or immigrants of some sort, as they had access to a wider selection of foods. The isotopes also revealed the presence of carbon, strontium, and oxygen, which confirms the growth of farming and agriculture. Together, this data implies that men would immigrate and marry into the agrarian societies, suggesting that women may have had relative power and high social status at the time.

After the Common Era - The Tais

While people existed in Thailand far before the Common Era, these people were not, in fact, "Tai" people. Although there is much debate on Thailand's original immigration patterns, the ancestors of the Thais, also referred to as the Tais, are believed to have come from southern China and/or northern Vietnam. Even before immigrating to the land now known as Thailand, as well as other Southeastern Asian countries, the earliest Tai populations, from around the 1st century CE, spoke Tai-Kadai, which is believed to have been Southeast Asia's largest ethnolinguistic group. For most of history, it was maintained that the Tais originated and lived in the valleys along the Yangtze River in China and that difficulties forced them to spread throughout Southeast Asia, eventually reaching Thailand. Now, many scholars and historians believe the Tais came from Dien Bien Phu, a city in northern Vietnam now known for the battles of the First Indochina War. The Tais, regardless of whether they originated from northern Vietnam or southern China, spread southward into Thailand and Laos, as well as to the north and west into China, Myanmar, Vietnam, and India. This would explain why there are large populations with Tai ancestors today, not just in Thailand but also in Laos, Myanmar, China, and Vietnam.

The Tai people are believed to have begun immigrating to Thailand around 1,000 years ago, where they mostly settled in the valleys along the country's rivers. Both before settling in what is now Thailand (dating back to the 1st millennium CE) and after, the Tais had a political organization, known as the müang, which consisted of many small groups of villages ruled by a common hereditary chief or lord, known as a chao. Historians believe that the strengths provided by this political system are what enabled the Tais to immigrate and expand through Southeast Asia as they did.

The Tais established their müangs in the valleys along Thailand's rivers, and their small settlements were agricultural-based communities. They very quickly began farming rice, fishing, foraging, and domesticating animals, such as pigs and fowl for eating and water buffalos for plowing. Over time, the Tais continued to expand their communities throughout Thailand, spreading from the northern valleys into central Thailand, which featured different landscapes than those they were used to, such as plains and plateaus. As the Tais immigrated southward from Vietnam and/or China, slowly populating Thailand, they came into contact with foreign empires and trading centers. The most notable of these foreign empires were the Mon-Khmer kingdoms, which had a major influence on the Tai people and, therefore, on the current Thai culture.

Mon-Khmer Civilizations

During the Tais' emigration to what is today Thailand, they came into contact with people of the Mon-Khmer ethnolinguistic groups. The Mon, similarly to the Tais (at least for much of history), were believed to have originated from China. The Mon spread southward throughout the north, west, and center of Thailand and southwest through Burma, or what is known as modern-day Myanmar. Since the Mon dominated most of what is now eastern Myanmar and west-central Thailand, they quickly established kingdoms centered around their religion of Theravada Buddhism. The first and most influential of these Mon kingdoms is known as Dvaravati, which was established surrounding the Chao Phraya River around the 6th century. Although the Mon inhabited Thailand as early as the 6th century, most modern-day Mon in Thailand were displaced from Burma between the 17th and 19th centuries.

The Khmer Empire was a well-developed polity, which was mostly established in modern-day Cambodia and which is often thought of as Southeast Asia's equivalent to the Roman Empire. Much like the Mon, the Khmer people mostly followed Theravada Buddhism, but they were once primarily based on Hinduism, and many still practiced it. The Khmer Empire's strength, power, and devotion to Hinduism can be attested by the enormous, extravagant temples built at the time. The most important and impressive of these was Angkor Wat, which was constructed in the 9th century in Cambodia. It is not only now a UNESCO World Heritage Site but also the world's largest religious monument by land area. Between the 9th and 13th centuries, the Khmer continued to expand westward from Angkor throughout Thailand, inhabiting mostly eastern Thailand along the Cambodian border. Despite the strength of the Khmer Empire, the majority of the current Khmer people in Thailand actually immigrated many years later after being displaced by wars, much like the Mon.

Throughout the 4th to 9th centuries, the Mon and Khmer populations continued to spread throughout Thailand, eventually coming into contact with the Tai immigrants between the 9th and 12th centuries. As the Tai soon became politically dominant (throughout the 13th century,) the Mon-Khmer populations displaced and assimilated into the Tai culture. Although the Mon-Khmer lost their power in Thailand, their influence is still evident and strong, both in Thailand's past and its modern-day national identity culture. The Tai combined their socio-political system, culture, and language with the Mons' religion and the statecraft and ceremonies of the Khmer to form the distinct Thai culture we know today.

Chapter 2 – Sukhothai Period (1238–1438)

Sukhothai before Thai Rule

Before the city of Sukhothai became the first capital of Thailand (which was then known as Siam) and the birthplace of much of Thai culture, it was, in fact, a Khmer city. Through the study of the still-standing ruins of Sukhothai, historians have theorized that the Khmers constructed Sukhothai at some point between the 12th century and early 13th century. This conclusion was drawn due to the similarities in design and structure with Angkor Wat and other Hindu temples built by the Khmer Empire at the time. The ancient city stood, and still remains, albeit in ruins, in the northeastern Sukhothai Province of Thailand. The impressive feats of design displayed in the city of Sukhothai not only share similarities but also rival those of Angkor Wat. Much like Angkor Wat, the city of Sukhothai is now revered for its sophisticated dams, canals, reservoirs, and other feats of hydraulic engineering. This advanced and sophisticated system, which permitted the city's future inhabitants to produce plentiful harvests and prevent droughts and flooding, certainly aided in the Sukhothai Kingdom's prosperity over the next 200 years.

Although the ruins of Sukhothai still displays evidence of the early Khmer Hindu-influenced construction, it now stands as a monumental Buddhist city, with influences from not only the Khmer but also the Mon and Tai as well. This is due to the immigrating patterns of the Tai people, who arrived in Sukhothai soon after the construction. They intermarried with the locals and formed müangs while remaining under Khmer rule. While the Tais did incorporate parts of the Khmer and Hindu culture into their own (which explains the Khmer influence on modern Thailand's culture), the Khmer Empire was overbearing and overruling. The Tais challenged Khmer authority and succeeded in gaining independence and conquering Sukhothai thanks to a combination of massive immigration, which reinforced the Tai population, and the already declining power of the Khmer Empire (this was due to a separate war throughout the late 12th and early 13th century).

Establishment of the Sukhothai Kingdom

The city was established by a Tai chieftain named Sri Indraditya in 1238. It was named Sukhothai, which quite literally translates to the "dawn of happiness." Following the victory over the Khmers, the Tais became known as the Thais, and the Sukhothai Kingdom was founded, with Sri Indraditya (taking the regnal name of Si Inthrathit) as its king. The word "Thai" was chosen to set the inhabitants of the Sukhothai Kingdom apart from the other Tai-speaking peoples scattered throughout Siam (Thailand), which was still under foreign rule.

King Si Inthrathit ruled the Sukhothai Kingdom, uniting the Thai müangs and leaders. Although Sukhothai remained a small power during his reign, King Si Inthrathit is revered and regarded as a sort of "founding father" of Thailand. King Si Inthrathit ruled Sukhothai until his death in 1270, when his first son, Ban Mueang, took over at a young age. Although much of the history preceding and during the 13th century is shrouded in mystery, historians do know for certain that Ban Mueang's rule was short-lived and that his brother, King Si

Inthrathit's second son, Prince Rama, took over the Sukhothai Kingdom in 1278.

King Ram Khamhaeng

It is when the third ruler of the Sukhothai Kingdom, Rama, took power that the kingdom truly grew and prospered. When Ram was only nineteen and still a prince, he aided his father in fighting off a raid from Khun Sam Chon, the ruler of Mae Sot, whom Rama fought in an elephant duel. Although many of Sukhothai's warriors fled, young Rama not only accepted the challenge but also beat Khun Sam Chon. Due to his bravery in battle, he earned the name Ram Khamhaeng, which translates to Rama the Bold (or Rama the Great.) Under King Ram Khamhaeng (also spelled as Ramkhamhaeng), the Thais grew to be the largest population in Siam.

Until its third ruler, Sukhothai had remained quite small, though it grew slowly and amounted some fortune. When King Ram Khamhaeng took the throne of Sukhothai in 1278, he continued to live up to his title of "Rama the Bold" and quickly expanded the Sukhothai Kingdom's influence to the rest of Thailand and Southeast Asia. Ram Khamhaeng extended the boundaries of the kingdom throughout Thailand from the northern city of Sukhothai to the southern Nakhon Si Thammarat. Ram Khamhaeng also expanded the territory and rule of the Sukhothai Kingdom into what is considered to be the modern-day Malay Peninsula, Laos, Myanmar, and Cambodia. He put Sukhothai on the map by establishing diplomatic relations and sending envoys to China, which was, at the time, ruled by the Yuan dynasty. These actions helped prompt trade between the two kingdoms, which encouraged and enriched the Sukhothai Kingdom's economy and influence.

Ram Khamhaeng did more than just expand the kingdom's territory. Under his rule, the city of Sukhothai flourished thanks to both its king and the city's convenient geographical location. Sukhothai finds itself in the north of Thailand, along the Yom River, between modern-day Myanmar and Cambodia. This meant that, at the time, the city of Sukhothai was about halfway between the Burmese Kingdom of Pagan and the Khmer Empire. Due to its convenient midway location, Sukhothai and its neighboring cities, also under the rule of Sukhothai, became profitable centers of production and commerce. The city of Si Satchanalai, which is only a mere 20 kilometers (12.5 miles) or so away from Sukhothai, became the kingdom's main ceramic production and exportation location. The neighboring countries' and kingdoms' demands, combined with Ram Khamhaeng's interest in art, led to the creation of unique pottery in Sukhothai and Si Satchanalai. The artisans of Sukhothai and Si Satchanalai developed a ceramic adorned with a green glaze, which attracted the attention of surrounding countries and spread throughout all of modern-day Southeast Asia. That being said, Sukhothai was not only a major trade city due to its admired ceramics and convenient location, as much of the city's prosperous commerce was due to its tax policies. Unlike many of the surrounding trade cities, the city of Sukhothai allowed people to trade with freedom, as no taxes were added on products.

Although the city of Sukhothai was built as a Khmer city, Buddhism was adopted as the kingdom's official religion during King Ram Khamhaeng's reign. By the end of the 13th century, the inhabitants of Sukhothai were not only devout Buddhists, but the city also became one of the world's largest Buddhist centers. Ram Khamhaeng's successors furthered his work in establishing Buddhism in the region by recruiting monks from other Buddhist nations and building Theravada Buddhist temples, many of which still stand to this day. The Sukhothai residents showed their devotion to Buddhism through art and architecture, developing a unique artistic and design style that spread and influenced future Buddhist images, statues, and temples.

One of King Ram Khamhaeng's greatest and most influential achievements during his lifetime was the creation of the Thai language. Ram Khamhaeng invented the language's writing system in 1283, which has remained mostly unchanged. This means that ancient writings from the 13th century can still be read by almost any Thai person today. One of the most important pieces of ancient writing, which comprises most of what we know about the 13th century today, is the inscription stone that was written by King Ram Khamhaeng himself in 1292. The King Ram Khamhaeng Inscription is an engraved four-sided pillar that tells of Ram Khamhaeng's life starting back at his birth, detailing his mother and father's names—Nang Suang and Sri Indraditya—and that he had four siblings. It is through the inscription stone that we know about the young death of Ban Mueang, Ram Khamhaeng's elder brother. He wrote of how the Sukhothai Kingdom spread throughout Southeast Asia, reaching Phrae and Nan in Thailand and Vientiane, Laos, to the north. He talked about the kingdom spreading to Nakhon Si Thammarat, the Mons' Hongsawadi, and the banks of the Mekong River in the south, east, and west, respectively. The inscription records the invention of the language, and it is the earliest example of Thai script, although Ram Khamhaeng used more words from the Khmer vocabulary than what is commonly used in Thai today. The inscription is split into three parts. The first mostly details Ram Khamhaeng's personal history, the second speaks of the city and kingdom of Sukhothai, and the last, which seems to have been written by a different person, glorifies the king after his death. Within the second portion, there are details of the Sukhothai Kingdom's views and values on religion, economy, politics, and law, much of which is not that far off from beliefs held around the world today.

Even though the Sukhothai Kingdom only existed between 1238 and 1438, a mere 200 years, it is quite literally the birthplace and backbone of modern Thailand's rich culture. The Sukhothai Kingdom's contemporary influence and impact are mostly thanks to

King Ram Khamhaeng, who invented the Thai language and officially adopted Buddhism, which allowed the religion to spread throughout the country. In addition to creating the country's language and adopting its religion, he also helped the kingdom flourish, leading to many important traditions and artistic and cultural advancements.

King Ram Khamhaeng died in 1298, and although the kingdom existed for around 140 more years, it steadily lost power after Ram Khamhaeng's death. After the passing of Ram Khamhaeng, the Sukhothai Kingdom was subsequently ruled by his son, Loe Thai. The throne was then usurped by Loe Thai's cousin, Ngua Nam Thum. He was followed by Li Thai (who is known as King Maha Thammaracha I). He was Loe Thai's son, making him the cousin of Ngua Nam Thum. The immediate rulers who followed King Ram Khamhaeng are mostly recognized for continuing to spread Theravada Buddhism throughout Thailand. Perhaps the most notable achievement of these kings is a text entitled *Sermon on the Three Worlds* (later known as *Three Worlds of King Ruang*), which was written by Li Thai, who, at the time, was the heir apparent to the Sukhothai Kingdom. The piece, which was written in 1345, is not only considered to be the first Thai literary work but also had such a major influence on Buddhism that some historians consider it to be the most important Thai text ever written.

Though the Sukhothai Kingdom's influence slowly declined following King Ram Khamhaeng's death, the straw that broke the camel's back was Phaya ("Lord") Maha Thammaracha I's passing in 1370. In addition to his death, which led to many satellite states withdrawing from the kingdom, the decline in Sukhothai Kingdom's power has been attributed to the establishment and strengthening of the Ayutthaya Kingdom, which was located not too far away in the south. Furthermore, it is believed that there were conflicts within the noble families and a decrease in the land's fertility, which would have also greatly influenced the decline of the Sukhothai Kingdom. In spite of the Sukhothai Kingdom's prosperity and affluence, they were challenged by King Borommarachathirat I of Ayutthaya. The once flourishing Kingdom of Sukhothai was forced to submit in 1378, and it was gradually annexed over the years into the Ayutthaya Kingdom. The Sukhothai Kingdom had two more kings following the annexation into the Ayutthaya Kingdom. In 1438, the once-great Kingdom of Sukhothai was finally completely absorbed by the Ayutthaya Kingdom.

Lan Na Kingdom

Although the Sukhothai Kingdom is regarded as the first, strongest, and largest Tai Kingdom in what is now modern-day Thailand, they were not the only Tai kingdom that reigned during this time. Another influential Tai kingdom was also formed during the 13th century, and it was called the Lan Na Kingdom. The Lan Na, which is another one of the first large Tai kingdoms to exist, and its capital city of Chiang Mai were founded in 1292 and 1296, respectively, by Mangrai. Similar to how Sukhothai was originally a Khmer city that was conquered by the Tai, Chiang Mai was originally a Mon city, known as Haripunjaya, which the Tai eventually conquered with Mangrai as their leader. Lan Na's power and influence grew with Mangrai and its subsequent rulers. It remained independent until the 16th century, just around 100 years after the fall of the Sukhothai Kingdom, when it was conquered by Burma (Myanmar). Although the Lan Na and Sukhothai Kingdoms had some contact during their reigns, specifically during an alliance made in 1287, the two kingdoms did not have much interaction at all. This is mostly due to the different cultures and languages that had developed in the two separate Tai kingdoms. While Theravada Buddhism was established as the Lan Na Kingdom's primary religion during Mangrai's rule, it wasn't until Tilokaracha, who took power in 1441, that Lan Na became a hub for the spread of Buddhism. Lan Na became known for its Theravada Buddhist literature and teachings, which spread Buddhism to the Tai people throughout Southeast Asia (including Myanmar and China).

Chapter 3 – Ayutthaya Period (1350–1767)

The Formation of the City of Ayutthaya

The city of Ayutthaya, located almost 350 kilometers (almost 220 miles) south of Sukhothai, was founded in 1350 by its first leader, a Tai named Ramathibodi I. While much of Ramathibodi I's life is unknown, it is believed that he was born in 1314 and was married to the daughter of the ruler of U Thong (which is now known as Suphan Buri). Ramathibodi I became the ruler of U Thong, explaining why he is now often referred to as simply U Thong. When Ramathibodi I took over U Thong in 1347, he moved the city eighty kilometers (about fifty miles) east to an island in the Chao Phraya River. The new city became known as Ayutthaya, which became the first capital city of Siam and remained the capital for over 400 years. The Ayutthaya Kingdom was actually the reason behind the country's original name, Siam, since the neighboring kingdoms and countries referred to the city and the Ayutthaya Kingdom population by this name.

Similar to the Sukhothai Kingdom, the Ayutthaya Kingdom benefited from their timing, as they immigrated to the city of Ayutthaya during the decline of the Khmer Empire. While the Tai, led by Ramathibodi I, gained power, they kept civil relations with the

Sukhothai Kingdom and focused their military energies against the Khmer Empire. Besides founding Ayutthaya, Ramathibodi I's greatest legacy was laying many of the foundations of the legal system that was used in Siam until the 1800s. Ramathibodi I spent many years preparing his son, Ramesuan, to take his throne, and he did so upon his passing in 1369. But soon after, power was taken by Borommaraja I (also spelled as Borommarachathirat). King Borommaraja I reigned Ayutthaya for eighteen years, in which time he challenged and seized the Sukhothai Kingdom, forcing them to partially annex with the Kingdom of Ayutthaya.

Borommaraja I's son, Thong Lan, inherited the throne in 1388, but his reign lasted for only seven days, during which time Ramesuan, Ramathibodi I's son, regained power. When King Ramesuan seized the throne from Borommaraja I's son, many were displeased, as Ramesuan was extremely unpopular. Power was instead given to his uncle, Prince Phangoa, known as Borommaracha I, who became the fifth king of Ayutthaya.

Ayutthaya cycled through many more kings, most notably Borommarachathirat II, who ruled during both the downfall of the Khmer Empire and the official absorption of the Sukhothai Kingdom. By the time Ayutthaya conquered the Khmer Empire, they had already expanded throughout parts of Southeast Asia, with their kingdom absorbing much of the former Khmer population. This led the Siamese Ayutthaya kings to adopt many of the Khmer's Hindu practices, most notably the concept of the *devarāja,* or divine king, which would give the king an almost god-like level of power. Under the belief of *devarāja,* the king could only be addressed in a special language and only be seen by the royal family. He also would have the power to sentence anyone in his kingdom to death.

Ayutthaya after the Absorption of Sukhothai

Borommatrailokanat, the eighth king of Ayutthaya, who is better known today as Trailok, ruled the kingdom between 1444 and 1488 when many of the first Hindu-influenced customs came into practice.

Trailok focused on centralizing Siam's political power by creating separate governmental departments that would be administered by workers rather than the royal family. These workers would be chosen by the king, who would select those who would help strengthen his administrative power. During Trailok's rule, a hierarchical system was introduced, similar to that of the caste system in India, which assigned *sakdi na* (unit or numerical rank) to the people in different social classes. Ranks within society were assigned based on the amount of land one possessed. The people of Ayutthaya were divided into royalty, nobility, and commoners. They would be further divided, more specifically within the commoners' category, into slaves and freemen. Although the hierarchy placed a clear separation between the classes, there was potential for social mobility through marriage or relations with someone of a higher class. The majority of the population of Ayutthaya, which found itself in the commoners' category, worked in the fields. Although they were not technically enslaved, the freemen still owed a "debt" to representatives of the king and were required to work for them six months of the year.

Despite Hinduism's strong influence on the Ayutthaya Kingdom, most of the population of Ayutthaya was devoutly Buddhist. The religion provided young male freemen with schooling, offering the opportunity for social mobility to those who wished to remain to learn within the Buddhist social order, known as the sangha.

Due to Ayutthaya's easily accessible location within the Chao Phraya River, which connected it to the Gulf of Thailand, the city became a major trade center. Its convenient location proved to be incredibly important during the century when European traders, beginning with the Portuguese in 1511, began traveling to Siam. The Portuguese were subsequently followed by the Dutch, English, Spanish, and French throughout the 17th century. They believed Ayutthaya to be the greatest and most prosperous of the Southeast Asian cities, if not of the world. Modern-day Thailand was put on the international map by King Narai of Ayutthaya, who invited travelers from all over to visit the city. European, Chinese, Indian, and Persian traders settled within Ayutthaya, establishing trading sites and employing missionaries. Furthermore, Ayutthaya sent out their own missionaries to spread Buddhism throughout Sri Lanka, China, and some of Europe. However, in 1688, the Siamese expelled the Europeans due to the pushy, overzealous French Christian missionaries.

The Burmese Conflicts

Despite all of these Western visitors, the Europeans did not pose any real threat to the Ayutthaya Kingdom other than perhaps the overzealous missionaries. Neither did the Asian countries of China, India, and Persia. The prosperous Ayutthaya Kingdom was, in fact, threatened by the Burmese state of Toungoo, which was rapidly rising and expanding in modern-day Myanmar. In the late 16th century, Bayinnaung, the king of Toungoo, helped the dynasty rise to become the most powerful Southeast Asian state. During his reign, he expanded the empire to Laos and finally to Siam, where Ayutthaya fell to the Burmese king in 1569. During the fifteen years following Burma's conquest of Ayutthaya, many Siamese inhabitants were deported as slaves, and those who remained saw their once-prosperous city pillaged.

At only sixteen years old, a Siamese boy named Naresuan was appointed as a vassal by the Burmese, replacing his father, Maha Thammaracha. In 1584, Naresuan recovered Siam's independence after leading a military operation in which he defeated Burmese armies and renounced his allegiance to Toungoo. Ayutthaya prospered once again under the reign of King Naresuan, who took the throne after his father passed in 1590. King Naresuan established the foundation for a strong Siam military force, which managed to not only seize the Cambodian capital, Lovek, but also resist the persisting Burmese conflicts. Almost all Burmese pressure on Siam ceased in 1593 after Naresuan defeated Burma's future prince. The Siam country and the Ayutthaya Kingdom continued to flourish and grow with subsequent kings.

The Ayutthaya Kingdom remained strong, resisting foreign threats while opening itself up internationally for almost two more centuries after Naresuan regained the country's independence in 1584. However, between the years of 1765 and 1767, the Ayutthaya Kingdom entered into a war with the Burmese Empire, known as the Burmese-Siamese War or "war of the second fall of Ayutthaya." As the latter title would indicate, in this battle, the 400-year-old Ayutthaya Kingdom finally fell, being conquered by the Burmese in 1767. Although the Siamese army was strong, the Burmese, led by King Hsinbyushin, invaded with a much larger army, which finally led to the final sacking of Ayutthaya. The battles devastated the city, leaving the once great Ayutthaya Kingdom in ruins. Almost all of the Ayutthaya art and records were burned, and most of the impressive feats of their early ancient architecture were completely destroyed. The majority of the Siamese warriors and people from the Ayutthaya Kingdom were wiped out, and those who survived, such as the royal family, were deported as captives to Burma. Though it was long ago, the impacts of the Burmese-Siamese War still plague relations between modern-day Myanmar and Thailand.

Chapter 4 – The Thon Buri Period (1767-1782)

The Aftermath of the Burmese Conflicts

After the fall of the Ayutthaya Kingdom in 1767, the once-prosperous city of Ayutthaya laid in ruins, and most of the Burmese soldiers who had aided in the pillaging and seizure of the city returned to what is considered to be modern-day Myanmar. Although a majority of the Ayutthaya civilians were killed in the battles or brought as captives to Burma, some Siamese managed to flee before the kingdom was brought to its knees. The remaining Ayutthaya people gathered into clans in the nearby provinces, but as they were now in need of a leader, those in charge of the clans, mostly the remaining governors and other men of importance, proceeded to fight to earn the title of king.

A former governor known as Taksin ended up emerging as the obvious leader and became the king of the remaining Ayutthaya people in 1767. Taksin was born in 1734 in the city of Ayutthaya to a Siamese (Thai) mother and a Chinese father. It is believed that Taksin was enrolled in government service and worked his way up to the rank of governor before the fall of the Ayutthaya Kingdom. During the Burmese battles, Taksin was called to help lead and defend the city and its kingdom from the Burmese threat. Although he and his troops fought alongside the Siamese soldiers in defense of Ayutthaya, it is believed that either late in the year 1766 or in early 1767, prior to the Burmese seizing the city, Governor Taksin and his troops left the capital and found safety in the surrounding provinces.

Settling in Thonburi

Once he was crowned, King Taksin began leading his followers downriver toward the east coast, traveling until they settled in Thonburi, around ninety kilometers (fifty-six miles) south of Ayutthaya. Throughout the whole journey, from their initial departure from Ayutthaya to their final destination of Thonburi, King Taksin and his troops ran into and defeated Burmese troops, earning King Taksin a reputation as a formidable military leader. As this reputation spread throughout the nearby provinces, many men joined King Taksin's troops, which helped to fortify his power and eventually the city of Thonburi.

King Taksin strategically chose to settle in Thonburi, which is just across the Chao Phraya River from modern-day Bangkok, since it would be difficult for the remaining Burmese troops to access while still having an accessible trade location. Upon the arrival of King Taksin and his troops, Thonburi was named the capital of Siam, and men from the surrounding provinces continued to join King Taksin's troops, which eventually turned into a powerful army. Not soon after arriving in Thonburi, King Taksin focused on collecting weapons, strengthening his army, and organizing a resistance to the Burmese invaders still remaining in the country. Once King Taksin had done this, he and his troops returned to Ayutthaya and managed to seize the city back from the Burmese in only two days. After the arduous Burmese rule in Siam, King Taksin drove the remaining Burmese out of the country, liberating Siam once again.

Although the country now known as Thailand was liberated, it was far from united. During the Burmese rule, the people of Siam had split into many factions, all of which were struggling and disorganized.

King Taksin conquered the factions, and by 1770, he had unified the country.

Although most of Taksin's accomplishments are military-related, the king did help to restart and rehabilitate the Thai economy. Thanks to King Narai's foreign relations prior to the fall of the city of Ayutthaya, the country already had developed trade relations with China. King Taksin capitalized on these existing relationships and invited craftsmen and merchants from China to settle in Thonburi. Not long after uniting the country of Siam, King Taksin restored the economy, thanks to the Chinese merchants and taxes he put in place. During his time as king, he also strengthened the trade relationships with European countries, such as Great Britain and the Netherlands. The king worked to develop Thonburi and had roads, canals, and temples built, renovated, and restored. During his reign, King Taksin also revived the arts in Thailand, focusing mainly on literature, since almost all of the previous Siamese works had been destroyed in the Burmese siege.

Although the Thonburi Kingdom only existed while King Taksin was on the throne, a mere fifteen years, this era remains one of Thailand's most expansive early periods. In 1769, not long after arriving and settling in Thonburi, King Taksin led his troops to conquer Korat, which is now Thailand's largest province, and Cambodia. In 1772, he returned to Cambodia and attacked once again to assert his power, replacing their king with a Cambodian prince of his choosing. In 1774, King Taksin annexed the city and the Lan Na Kingdom, which had been around since the Sukhothai period but had been seized by the Burmese, and the city was absorbed into the Thonburi Kingdom. By 1776, King Taksin had absorbed almost all of the tribes in Thailand and had truly united the country that had been mostly made of smaller separate factions. By the end of King Taksin's reign, Siam and the Thonburi Kingdom had expanded to include much of modern-day Thailand, the Malay Peninsula, Laos, and Cambodia.

The End of King Taksin's Reign

However, despite all of King Taksin's accomplishments and achievements during his fifteen-year reign as the king of Siam and Thonburi, in 1782, he was forced to step down and was executed. It is said that at the beginning of the 1780s, King Taksin began to lose his mind, and many documents speak of his, what we would now refer to, mental instability. Apparently, King Taksin started to believe he was advancing toward Buddhahood and tried to force the belief of his divinity onto his followers. These actions led to rebellions and dissatisfaction amongst the united Siam people, so much so that King Taksin came close to undoing all that he had achieved during his reign. The country of Thailand and the Kingdom of Siam would have likely crumbled had it not been for a revolution that broke out in Bangkok, with his ministers eventually deciding to have him executed. King Taksin was replaced in 1782 by Chao Phraya Chakri, who was a governor and chief campaigning in Cambodia at the time. Chao Phraya Chakri would later be known as "Great Lord" Rama I and the founder of the Chakri dynasty.

Although Taksin's reign was short-lived, and he was, in the end, dethroned and executed, he is regarded as a hero in Thai history. During his fifteen-year reign, he rid the country of the Burmese threat, which had destroyed the Ayutthaya Kingdom and caused so much suffering to the people of Siam. He also united the country of Siam and expanded its borders to include much of today's modern Thailand. These, along with many of his other accomplishments, are why he is referred to today as "King Taksin the Great." On December 28th, the date he was crowned as the king of Siam in 1767, is celebrated in Thailand as King Taksin Day. There is a shrine erected at Wat Lum Mahachai Chumphon, where the king is said to have stopped on his way to free Ayutthaya from Burmese control. Today, many, including both Thai locals and Chinese visitors, go there to pray on King Taksin Day.

Chapter 5 – The Beginning of the Chakri Dynasty (1782–1868)

Reign of Rama I (r. 1782-1809)

Following the arrival of King Taksin and his people in Thonburi, Chao Phraya Chakri joined and moved his way up in King Taksin's troops until achieving the high leadership position of military commander of the northern provinces. During the Thonburi period, he led Thai troops in Laos, Cambodia, and the Malay states and was regarded as one of Taksin's most exemplary generals. He was actually on a campaign in Cambodia when the rebellions against Taksin were beginning to take place, and he was called back to take his place at the beginning of 1782. He was crowned as the new king on April 6th of that year and became known as Rama I, Phra Phutthayotfa Chulalok ("the Buddha on top of the sky and the crown of the worlds"). He would be the first of his family to rule, and his descendants would continue to reign the country now known as Thailand, with Rama X of the Chakri dynasty recognized as the king of Thailand today.

One of Rama I's first moves as king was to move the capital of the country from Thonburi to Bangkok, which, of course, is still the capital of Thailand today. Bangkok was mostly undeveloped at the time and was, in comparison with Thonburi or Ayutthaya, still a small village. King Rama I had new infrastructures built, with palaces and Buddhist temples constructed in a very similar elaborate style as the Ayutthaya designs. Through establishing these somewhat grandiose temples, Rama I was able to restrengthen the Buddhist religion throughout the country. During his reign, he requested to have many of the essential Buddhist texts translated to Thai, which helped to establish the sangha, which refers to the monastic order in Buddhism.

Rama I also focused on restoring Thailand's cultural arts and heritage, much of which had been lost during the Burmese pillaging of Ayutthaya. This was made easier due to the fact that Rama I's predecessor, King Taksin, had already attempted to revive some of the artistic cultural customs. Rama I had many works of literature brought from other countries, namely India and China, in addition to others, and he strongly encouraged the citizens of Bangkok to reinterest themselves in the arts, which certainly helped lay the foundation for much of Thailand's cultural arts and heritage throughout history and today.

Although King Taksin had driven out the Burmese troops from Siam during the Thonburi period, the Burmese kingdom would continue to threaten the country following Rama I's move to Bangkok. They would be a threat until 1820, when the British army would force Burmese troops to return to their home country and defend their kingdom. The first Burmese attack during Rama I's reign occurred in 1785. It was a massive invasion, and Rama I's troops were barely able to fight it off. Although it was difficult, the Siamese troops managed to repel the Burmese attacks in 1785, as well as those attacks in 1786, 1787, 1797, and 1801, although these later ones were on a much smaller scale. King Rama I would continue to strengthen his troops and expand the kingdom throughout Southeast Asia. By the beginning of the 1800s, under the reign of Rama I as well as Rama II, the Chakri dynasty had extended its power to much of Laos, Cambodia, and Vietnam.

Toward the end of Rama I's twenty-seven-year reign, he published Thailand's first written form of law and issued comprehensive court law codes and court rituals. This codification of law, which was completed in 1805, was adapted from laws that date as far back as King Ram Khamhaeng from the Sukhothai Kingdom. That being said, many of the laws crystalized by Rama I were ones set in place throughout the Ayutthaya period, and they were derived from both Hindu and Buddhist practices. This set of revised written laws were known as the *Three Seals Law*, and it would remain almost completely unaltered until the reign of Rama V in 1882. Rama I reigned as the first king of the Chakri dynasty until his death in 1809. He would be succeeded by his son, who would be known as Rama II.

Reign of Rama II (r. 1809-1824)

Rama II, also known as Phraphutthaloetla Naphalai, was the second ruler of the Chakri dynasty. His reign was fairly short, lasting only 15 years, and during that time, he aided in the reconstruction of Thailand's cultural arts, heritage, and traditions. Rama was enamored with the arts, specifically poetry, and it was under his reign that the great Thai poet Sunthon Phu wrote some of his most influential works, which are regarded as some of Thailand's best works of poetry ever written. Rama II was also himself a gifted artist. During his lifetime, he wrote many famous poems, such as a well-known dramatic rendition of Inao and Sang Thong, which is a popular dance drama.

Although King Taksin had maintained relations with China, most of Thailand's foreign relations had been closed off since the rule of King Narai during the Ayutthaya period. Under Rama II's rule, Siam reconnected with the West, namely Portugal in 1818 and Great Britain in 1822.

During King Rama II's rule, Thailand would see its first outbreak of cholera, a disease that would continue to plague the country for years to come. The first case in Thailand dates back to 1820. To attempt to fight the plague, King Rama II ordered the population to stay home from work and to focus on observing their Buddhist practices. This stay-at-home decree helped in ridding the country of cholera for the time being. Despite the fact that King Rama's royally ordered quarantine eventually worked, it is estimated that likely around 30,000 people died from the outbreak.

Rama II would rule Thailand from his father's death in 1809 until his own death in 1824, and he would be succeeded by his son, who would come to be known as Rama III. In comparison to his father's rule, Rama II's time as king was mostly peaceful, which allowed him to focus much of his energy on reviving the arts and culture in Siam, laying the further foundation for Thailand's rich arts and culture today.

Reign of Rama III (r. 1824-1851)

Rama III's succession to the throne is considered to be somewhat of a strange and rare occurrence. His father, Rama II, as with most Thai royalty during this era, had many concubines—in other words, a lover with a lower status than a wife—in addition to his wife, who was the queen of Siam until her husband's death. Rama III, also known as Nangklao, was born on March 31st, 1788, in Bangkok to one of Rama II's concubines. Although Rama II had a legitimate son, Prince Mongkut, Nangklao (Rama III) was chosen to rule upon his father's death instead.

This strange choice by the accession council was due to the fact that from a young age, Nangklao (Rama III) was put in charge of overseeing the country's foreign trade and relations, which made him more experienced than his brother. This experience would explain why much of what is written and remembered about Rama III's reign is related to foreign relations.

Throughout the beginning of the Chakri dynasty, Britain had been increasingly threatening the Burmese kingdom, which was to the benefit of Siam, as it had been battling with the Burmese for many centuries by this point. It was not until Britain increased their military in what is now modern-day Myanmar that the Burmese stopped being a threat to the Chakri dynasty. War was finally declared between Britain and the Burmese kingdom in 1824, and its proximity to Siam left Rama III fearful that the powerful British army might eventually attack his kingdom as well. This thinking led Rama III to agree to sign the 1826 Burney Treaty, which mostly covered trade and economic agreements. The British had failed to get King Rama II to sign this agreement in 1822, as he was certainly less open to the West than his successor. The Burney Treaty would finally permit English tradesmen to operate in Bangkok; however, the treaty had quite limited clauses and high taxes, which would lead to a stricter treaty being put in place later in 1855, after Rama III's death.

Although diplomatic relations had been established between Thailand and the United States, likely by Rama III when he was overlooking the country's foreign relations, no official agreements were signed between the two countries until 1833. That year, the United States and Thailand signed the Treaty of Amity and Commerce, with the very first article claiming the two countries shall have perpetual peace. The other nine articles in the treaty essentially laid out commerce and trade regulations, such as citizens of the United States having free liberty to enter Siam through its ports to sell and purchase in the country's many markets. This agreement is actually the United States of America's very first treaty of any kind made with any Asian country. The treaties between the Kingdom of Siam and the United States, as well as between Great Britain, which were mainly put in place to allow foreign merchants to buy and sell in Siam, would greatly impact Thailand's infrastructures throughout the rest of history.

Rama III's reign would also lead to further strengthening of the Siamese army. Throughout the 1830 and 1840s, under Rama III's lead, the Kingdom of Siam continued to establish and assert their military dominance throughout Southeast Asia, specifically in Cambodia and Laos, where they fought to defend the two aforementioned countries from the Vietnamese. This period also marked a change between Siam and Kedah, now Malaysia, which Siam had been occupying since the start of the 19th century. In 1837, following Rama III's mother's death, many of the officials stationed in Kedah returned to Siam. This space allowed Kedah to finally accomplish what they had been trying to do for over a decade already, which was to launch a rebellion in 1838 against the Siamese. Following the rebellion, in 1839, the Kingdom of Siam realized any further direct involvement in Kedah would lead to more resistance, so Kedah became mostly autonomous, with the two kingdoms entering into a peaceful coexistence.

Much like during his father's and grandfather's reigns, art was of great importance during Rama III's reign. What is unique to Rama III is the amount of outside influence that impacted Thai art. In addition to the numerous Western influences that are obvious within Thai art from this time, the Chinese, who had been inhabiting the Kingdom of Siam throughout the entire Chakri dynasty, also had a great amount of influence. Much of this Chinese influence can be seen in the temple paintings from this time.

Rama III is widely remembered for his accomplishments in foreign relations, which helped put Thailand on the global map and extending its trade all the way to North America. He ruled from his father's death in 1824 until his own death in 1851. Although King Rama III never took a wife, he had fifty-one children. However, seeing as none of them were born in wedlock, in addition to the fact that he never named a successor, the throne finally went to Prince Mongkut, the son of King Rama II and his wife, Queen Sri Suriyendra.

Reign of Rama IV (r. 1851-1868)

Mongkut, also known as Rama IV or by his reigning title, Phra Chom Klao Chao Yu Hua, was born in 1804 and was the first son of King Rama II and his wife, Queen Sri Suriyendra. Although he was the first in line to take the throne after his father's death in 1824, seeing as Mongkut was only twenty in 1824, the throne was instead given to his half-brother, who became known as Rama III. Instead of becoming a military general or working in the royal government, Mongkut became a Buddhist monk, and an accomplished one at that. At the monastery, Mongkut made connections with Christians from both the United States and France, which would lead to enhancing both the West's understanding of Buddhism and the Thais' understanding of Western languages and advancements in the sciences.

During Mongkut's twenty-seven years in a Bangkok monastery, he helped to develop Thai Buddhism into what it is today. While at the monastery, Mongkut was concerned that many of the techniques and practices taught to him were superstitious and strayed away from Buddha's original teachings. Mongkut sought to purify Buddhism once again, and he found more of what he was looking for while traveling to the countryside and encountering Siam's remaining Mon, who practiced stricter Buddhist disciplines than the Siamese people. Inspired by the many practices he picked up from the Mon, Mongkut would go on to found the Thammayut order, which is now one of Thailand's two main Theravada Buddhism denominations.

After spending twenty-seven years in the monastery, Mongkut, also known as Rama IV, took his rightful place as the king of Siam after his half-brother's death in 1851. During Rama IV's reign, he continued to strengthen Buddhism throughout the country. However, he is likely best remembered for his foreign relations. Following Rama III's somewhat restrictive treaties with Britain, in 1855, the queen of England sent Sir John Bowring to demand that the treaties be reestablished and less restrictive. Considering Britain had waged wars on other countries for restrictive treaties, Siam signed the Bowring Treaty in April 1855, which gave the British diplomatic immunity in Siam and removed the tariffs and duties placed on foreigners. Similar revised agreements were also signed between Siam and other European countries, as well as the United States, between 1855 and 1870.

Though King Rama IV's signing of the Bowring Treaty and other subsequent agreements protected Siam's sovereignty, it greatly damaged the kingdom's economy and independence. This forced the king to find other sources of revenue, which led to crops being planted to sell in global markets, canal systems being built to help with exporting goods, and an increase in taxes. In the end, the treaties Rama IV signed did more good than harm since they helped create rapid growth in Siam's economy, put Siam firmly on the global map, and prevent wars that other neighboring rulers had fought due to not adjusting their original restrictive treaties made with the Western countries.

Although the Bowring Treaty was mostly centered around foreign trade, it certainly led to an overall increase of foreign influences on Siam. Prior to the treaties, Siam was ruled by a very strict sovereignty, and though Siam was still ruled by a monarchy following the Bowring Treaty, that strict, uncompromising authoritarian sovereignty would no longer be possible if Siam was to accommodate for the new Western influences. Under King Rama IV, Siam's view of the monarchy became less traditionally strict and more modern, which would strip the royal order of some of their powers but overall prevent any rebellions or wars within the country or with any foreign nations.

Another example of the change brought by the increase in foreign influence was the introduction of Western ideas in Siam's education. European countries once again began sending missionaries to attempt to convert the Thais into Christians, and although they were unsuccessful, they did end up building medical facilities and other Western-styled infrastructures. It was actually American Protestant missionaries that brought over the first printing press and ended up creating Thailand's first newspaper.

Rama IV ensured his children had access to Western advisors, teachers, and tutors who would help enhance their understanding of the changing world. Mongkut brought in French missionaries to teach his kids Latin, math, and astronomy, as well as an American missionary to teach them English. One of these tutors was Anna Harriette Leonowens, a teacher from Britain. Her life would be made into a novel called *Anna and the King of Siam,* which would later be made into the well-known musical *The King and I.* These works were widely popular in the Western world, and despite being riddled with inaccuracies, they would shape much of the West's understanding of Thailand, much to the Kingdom of Siam's dismay. Both of these works are considered to be highly controversial in Thailand, so much so that the book was banned in the country. Even today, theatrical versions of the book are often banned in Thailand due to historical inaccuracies. Anna Harriette Leonowens claims that she greatly influenced Mongkut's son, who would go on to become Rama V; however, it is debated exactly how much impact she had on the future king.

Rama IV ruled the Kingdom of Siam until his death in 1868, and he was succeeded by his son. Rama IV's time as king would mark many changes in Thailand's culture, namely the modernization of the sovereignty and the ceding of many of the royal order's powers. He is remembered for his creation of the currently widely popular Buddhist Thammayut order, but he is perhaps most remembered for introducing many Western ideas, concepts, and infrastructures into the country, which laid the foundation for Thailand's unique culture.

Chapter 6 – The Modernization of Thailand and the Reign of the Great Rama V (1868–1910)

Although King Mongkut was succeeded by his son Chulalongkorn, who would come to be known as Rama V, Chulalongkorn was barely sixteen at the time of his father's death in 1868 and not prepared to run the Kingdom of Siam. Chulalongkorn spent the subsequent five years following King Rama IV's death traveling to neighboring European-colonized countries and observing political and judicial proceedings in preparations to fully take the throne. During this time, a notable minister named Somdet Chao Phraya Si Suriyawong, also known by his personal name Chuang Bunnag, whose family had held important posts since the 17th century, was appointed as the regent. Chuang Bunnag was one of the highest-ranking officials under King Mongkut and had been a key player in the Kingdom of Siam's treaties with the Western countries. Since Chuang Bunnag was such a powerful official under the previous king's reign, he was extremely adept at running the kingdom, and in 1873, when Chulalongkorn was prepared to take the lead, Chuang Bunnag remained as an official and advisor until his death in 1883.

An accurate way of describing Chulalongkorn's ruling style would be "like father like son." In comparison to the kings of the Ayutthaya Kingdom or even the early Chakri dynasty, who didn't allow people of the lower class to see them or look at their face and ruled with god-like power, Rama V (Chulalongkorn) acted more similarly to a modern politician. Rama V went out in public dressed casually (or at least casually in comparison to what kings would normally be seen wearing), and he would allow his face to be printed and reproduced on products such as coins and stamps, which no previous king had allowed before. Although Rama IV had taken great strides to modernize the Kingdom of Siam, it is Rama V who is remembered for defying the outdated traditions and modernizing the country.

Similar to his father, Chulalongkorn focused much of his time on foreign relations. Although previous kings of Siam had made connections and agreements with foreign countries through missionaries and merchants sent to Thailand, King Rama V would travel to countries throughout Europe and Southeast Asia. These trips and the trips taken before his reign while he was preparing to take the throne would inspire King Rama V. These inspirations are demonstrated in ornate European-style structures built during his reign, which would have been similar to what he had seen on his trips, as well as in his choice to defy the traditional practices in Thailand and conduct many modernizing political reforms.

Almost immediately after Chulalongkorn fully took over power at the age of twenty, he began to put in place a series of significant reforms in the country's law, finance, and political structures, much of which were drawn from Western models he had observed while preparing to lead. Unlike the previous kings of Siam, who had relied almost exclusively on the advice of their Siamese officials, King Rama V had many foreign advisors, the majority of which were from Britain. Rama V felt that it was important that all future royalty attend Western-style schools to prepare for their futures in leading positions and that all promising future government and military officials should study in Europe.

Between 1868 and 1910, the country experienced rapid modernization. King Rama V very quickly laid out a new political order and a more comprehensive legal system and legal code, putting a stop to arbitrary laws. He pushed for primary education and enforced military conscription, which together created the foundation of what it meant to be a citizen in the Kingdom of Siam. This, along with the abolition of slavery and state labor, were all accomplished within the first few years of his reign. In 1892, all of these actions led to the separation of the government into twelve ministries, three of which were defense, education, and justice, which is not too dissimilar to the political structures we see today. It was under Rama V that the Kingdom of Siam introduced a police force, a government-run currency-based tax collection, and a modern school system. Although Thailand had been a unified country before King Rama V, the Kingdom of Siam developed a centralized administration that would connect all of its provinces. Finally, as another sign of modernization, Siam began constructing railways, which were finished in 1897 (and extended during the subsequent years), connecting Bangkok and Ayutthaya and, in 1903, to connect to the British Malaysian railroads.

While all of these reforms were happening internally, many of which were due to Western influence, the Kingdom of Siam was gradually losing territory to these same Western countries. Similar to agreements made by King Mongkut with the Western countries, King Rama V skillfully signed agreements that, despite reducing the Kingdom of Siam's independence and landmass, helped the country avoid Western colonization. In 1893, the Kingdom of Siam ceded all Lao territories that they had been occupying east of the Mekong River to France. Similar agreements were made in 1907 when Thailand ceded their landmass in Cambodia to France and in 1909 when they ceded many Malayan states to Britain.

All things considered, despite the land they were ceding to Western countries, Thailand kept its independence and was being globally established as a powerful force. To celebrate Thailand's freedom in contrast to its colonized neighbors, in 1902, the country unofficially became known as *Prathet Thai* or *Ratcha Anachak Thai*, which translates, respectively, to the "country of the free" and the "kingdom of the free." The country's name was not officially changed to Thailand until 1939.

Seeing as Chulalongkorn (Rama V) began his rule so young, succeeding his father in 1868 at the age of sixteen, and ruling until he died in 1910, he had one of the longest reigns in the country's history. Although his extended reign explains how he was able to achieve so much during his time as king, overall, the rapid modern reforms that Rama V introduced into Thailand were completely unprecedented. King Rama V is remembered as one of Thailand's greatest, most successful, and most notable kings.

Chapter 7 – The Final Absolute Monarchs of Thailand (1910–1932)

The Reign of King Rama VI (r. 1910–1925)

King Rama V's successor was his son Vajiravudh, who later became known as Rama VI. Vajiravudh went to Oxford University, making him the first king of Siam to ever have a foreign education. Prior to ruling Siam, he also served in the British army, but he only did so briefly, as he returned home in 1903 after being named his father's successor to prepare himself for the throne, which he would take after his father's death in 1910.

King Rama VI's time spent in Europe greatly impacted many of his social reforms. During his reign, he recodified Siamese law and introduced many Western-inspired laws, banning polygamy and ordering all citizens to adopt surnames. Although some of his Westernized changes were beneficial to the country, such as the creation of the Thai Red Cross, other changes were of less significance, such as the introduction of the Gregorian calendar. However, many civilians felt King Rama VI pushed the Westernization of Thailand too far. One example of this would be when he strongly suggested that the Siamese stop wearing traditional Thai garb and adopt a more European-style of clothing.

Considering King Rama VI was not only the first ruler of Thailand to have a foreign education (he was also the first one to attend university), it comes as no surprise that during his reign, he greatly aided in advancing the education system. In 1917, almost two decades after returning home from Oxford University, he founded and opened the first university in Thailand, which he named Chulalongkorn University after his father. Although the building was constructed under his father's reign for instructing government workers, under King Rama VI, it became a proper university. Chulalongkorn University, which is still located in Bangkok, is considered to be one of the top fifty universities in all of Asia and the number one institute of higher education in Thailand today. To also aid in advancing the country's education, Vajiravudh (King Rama VI) would continue to push his father's enforcement of primary school for children, and in 1921, he would officially make primary school education compulsory and free for everyone in Thailand.

Ever since King Narai's rule during the Ayutthaya period, Thailand had a large population of Chinese people, not all of which understood Thai or connected with the Siamese culture. King Rama VI not only passed laws forcing compulsory primary school but also an act that everyone in the country had to learn the Thai language. In his quest for nationalism, he sought that all students would learn the language until they were fluent and also be educated on Siamese culture and national duties.

Under King Rama VI, the Kingdom of Siam had access to arts and scientific and technological advancements of other countries around the world, which would help Thailand rapidly modernize at the same pace as the other connected countries. When the country was faced with smallpox, they had access to the British-invented smallpox vaccine, and King Rama VI was able to implement a universal dose of the vaccine to every citizen in Thailand. King Rama VI also established Thailand's very own Red Cross. Although the humanitarian organization was technically around during his father's reign, it was under Vajiravudh that it became recognized by the International Red Cross Committee. King Rama VI also attempted to crack down on Thailand's drug problems, specifically opium, which affected and other neighboring and international countries, which were also seeking solutions to the problem around this same time.

That being said, King Rama VI's globally-accessed advancements weren't only scientific and humanitarian. King Rama VI was also known as a patron of the arts and spent much of his spare time translating international works into Thai. He translated hundreds of famous plays and books, including many of Shakespeare's, introducing Thailand to many Western works of art that weren't previously accessible. On top of translations, King Rama VI wrote dozens of original plays and dramas, almost all of which under pseudonyms and many of which are still beloved in the country today. King Rama VI wrote many of his works, although not all, surrounding the topic of nationalism, a concept that deeply fascinated him. After spending so much time in the West, King Rama VI often compared and contrasted the facets of Thai and Western nationalism, many concepts he would then introduce into his politics.

King Rama VI ruled between 1910 and 1925, which means he oversaw the country during World War I. The Kingdom of Siam fought on the side of the Allies and sent troops to fight alongside them in Europe. In the end, this action certainly aided the Kingdom of Siam in its foreign relations with European countries, namely Britain and France. Fighting alongside the Allies also meant that when the war ended, the Kingdom of Siam was able to bring home the spoils of winning a war, which included an arsenal of German ships. Under King Rama VI, in 1919, Siam attended the peace conference in Versailles and was one of the founding countries of the League of Nations. Following the war, due to both the Kingdom of Siam's strengthened European relations and Europe's loss in power, King

Rama VI was able to persuade the Western countries to cede their extraterritorial rights in the country. This would mean that all Western travelers would have to follow local laws and would no longer be granted immunities when they were in the Kingdom of Siam.

King Rama VI never truly struck the right balance between Western ideologies and conserving Thai culture. Although he strongly promoted Thai nationalism, his Western ideas of nationalism with utility in mind led to a great reluctance amongst the civilians. An example of this was when King Rama VI tried to create the Wild Tiger Corps, a military force that was separate from the country's army and under King Rama VI's direct command. This royal paramilitary force resembled the royally-run armies in Britain at the time. This, coupled with the other English and European traditions that King Rama VI was trying to push on the country's people, led to a disgruntled population. Many were offended by his choices and saw them as undermining Thai culture and Siamese heritage rather than modernizing the country as he was intending. Public opinion of King Rama VI was not helped by the fact that (toward the end of his reign especially) he was overspending and leading the country into economic issues. This resentment was shared amongst the corps, and in 1912, some navy and army officials began to plot a rebellion of sorts to restrict the king's power. Although the plan was aborted, the population of Siam remained wary and resentful of the king, as well as the next king. King Rama VI died in 1925, and the throne was succeeded by his brother, Prajadhipok (King Rama VII), who inherited a disgruntled population no longer satisfied with the country's absolute monarchy.

The Reign of King Rama VII (r. 1925-1935)

Generally, a reigning king will choose an heir to the throne many years before the end of his reign, with some successors being chosen from birth and others being decided upon when they become of age and showed potential. Either way, a successor is typically given enough years to prepare for leadership through observing and working their way up in other government. This was not the case for Vajiravudh's brother Prajadhipok, who never expected to be king. Similar to his brother, Prajadhipok had a foreign education, but unlike his brother, Prajadhipok had been attending school to prepare for a career in the military. Prajadhipok, who was also known as Phrapokklao and who would later be known as King Rama VII, attended Eton College, which is an all-boys boarding school for those aged thirteen to eighteen. Founded by Henry VI, Eton College is globally considered one of the most prestigious schools for this specific age range. Following his time at Eton College, Prajadhipok attended the Woolwich Royal Military Academy to further his military training, meaning that a large portion of his teenage and young adult life was spent outside of Thailand, with access to more Western influences and ideologies than his brother. At the beginning of 1925, not even a year before the throne would be passed to him, he became the most likely successor to the throne, even though, unlike the previous kings, he did not have years of preparation or governmental experience. Prajadhipok was only officially and formally announced as the successor to the throne on November 24th, 1925, only two days before his brother would pass.

When King Prajadhipok (Rama VII) began his reign, he inherited a discontent population and some significant financial issues. Due to his brother's extravagant spending, King Rama VII was forced to lay off a good amount of government officials within the first year of his reign. Although the layoffs helped stave off the Kingdom of Siam's fiscal issues for a few years, at the start of the 1930s, Thailand and the rest of the world would be hit with the Great Depression. The Great Depression would force King Rama VII to lay off even more government officials, cutting workers from every ministry and department. At the same time, the resentment many of the middle-class civilians had held during King Rama VI's reign had only grown stronger. With the combination of the dissatisfied working middle-class civilians and now the disgruntled laid-off government officials and the government officials' families, discontentment with the absolute monarchy became the popular opinion. Backed by the majority of the population, newspapers and other media began shining a light and giving voices to the dissatisfied people.

Of course, with all of the press coverage, King Rama VII was aware of the population's growing resentment of the royal family and of the absolute monarchical government. The king was rightfully convinced that he would need to begin moving toward political reforms that would introduce democratic practices, ones that would lessen the royal family's power and give more power to the people. Considering King Rama VII, like his brother, had spent many years in the West, he was open to moving toward a more democratic political system. However, despite his own convictions, the senior and more experienced royal court members did not agree with him. Although these senior government officials certainly restrained him, King Rama VII did not push hard for change, and though he believed that the government needed reforms, he remained outwardly ignorant toward his people's demands. It would be this inactivity in the face of the population's complete dissatisfaction with absolute sovereignty that led to the Thai (or Siamese) revolution of 1932.

The Thai Revolution of 1932

Although a good majority of the Thai population was dissatisfied with the absolute monarchy by the beginning of the 1930s, the Thai revolution of 1932 was actually started by a group of young Thai students who had studied abroad. In fact, they actually began plotting the revolution while living and studying in Europe. The revolutionary movement, known as Khana Ratsadon, or the People's Party, was led by Pridi Phanomyong and Plaek Khittasangkha, better known as Phibun to Western audiences.

Pridi Phanomyong was born in Ayutthaya, Siam, in 1900, making him only thirty-two years old at the time of the Thai revolution of 1932. Born to a Thai mother and a Chinese father, Pridi excelled in school from a young age. His father was a rice merchant, but rather than following in his father's footsteps, Pridi put his time and effort into making his way through school. His dedication to a solid education paid off, as he graduated from secondary school at only fourteen years old, four years ahead of the typical graduation age, and completed law school at the Thai Royal College of Law by the time he was nineteen. He was a shining pupil, and although he was many years younger than his peers, he was awarded a scholarship to the University of Caen in France to study law. He subsequently attended the University of Paris to earn his doctorate. By the time Pridi Phanomyong was twenty-seven, he had graduated with a masters in law and economics and a doctorate in law. The air of revolution was not only present in his home of Siam but also in France as well. Pridi Phanomyong's time in Paris allowed him to observe and take part in the radical revolutionary movements that would help shape France's democratic politics. While in France, Pridi would not only be inspired by the revolutionary socialistic and democratic movements and politics in the country, but he would also meet Major Plaek Khittasangkha, and together they would form the Khana Ratsadon (the People's Party).

Plaek Khittasangkha was born in 1897 in a province north of Bangkok. Plaek Khittasangkha was raised to join the military and would attend the Chulachomklao Royal Military Academy, a military school located in one of Thailand's central provinces. In 1914, at only seventeen years old, Plaek Khittasangkha graduated from the academy and was sent to the artillery, commissioned as a second lieutenant. He spent around a decade in the Siamese artillery corps, where he displayed outstanding natural military instincts, prowess, and intelligence. Plaek Khittasangkha's excellent military performance was rewarded in 1924 when he was sent to advance his military training in France. Plaek would continue to study artillery tactics in France between 1924 and 1927, and in 1928, after returning to Bangkok, he was promoted to major, receiving the title *Luang*. As a result of this, he began going by the name Luang Phibunsongkhram (better known as Phibun to Western audiences). Similar to his future revolutionary counterpart Pridi Phanomyong, it was in France that Phibun began to realize the need for political reforms in the Kingdom of Siam and the power of a people-run revolution. During his time studying in France, Phibun would come into contact with Pridi Phanomyong and many other Thai students who were studying abroad and who were discontent with the Kingdom of Siam's politics.

While there are many factors that led to the Thai revolution of 1932, or as it was called then the Siamese Revolution of 1932, many historians and participants agree that the revolution unfolded as it did due to King Rama V's policies to send students to receive foreign educations. As we saw with King Rama VI and King Rama VII, who both had foreign educations in England, they both became infatuated with Western ideologies. However, unlike King Rama VI and King Rama VII, who were, of course, from the royal family and quite wealthy, the non-royal students being sent to Europe and elsewhere were not as privileged, and they shared similar views on the monarchy as the rest of the country's working-class civilians.

Throughout King Rama VII's reign, the number of scholarships given out by the government to talented non-royal family men significantly increased. Ironically enough, by sending students to study abroad, Thailand's absolute monarchist government was essentially giving out the education that led to its undoing. What awaited the students who studied in foreign countries were lessons of Western democratic politics and freedoms. As Thai students continued to attend foreign schools and connect with one another while abroad, they discussed politics and came to realize that the absolute monarchy in their home country was not only unsatisfying but was also growing to become intolerable.

The number of students from the Kingdom of Siam attending schools in Western countries continued to increase throughout the 1920s, and by the 1930s, it is assumed that there were at least a couple hundred Thai students spread throughout England, France, the

United States, the Philippines, and other European countries. Although the students were mostly sent to these countries to get a better understanding of Western practices that could help modernize the Kingdom of Siam, many, though not all, of the students would bring home revolutionary democratic political ideas. Rather than bringing home techniques to help advance the absolute monarchy's political system, many of the students came to the conclusion that the monarchy would have to be entirely replaced by democracy, as they believed this would be the only way to truly modernize the country.

While attending school in France to earn his masters and doctorate in law, Pridi Phanomyong became the secretive face of the revolutionary and somewhat anarchist Thai student movement. Since there were so many Thai students in France, there was already an association of Thai students in France, of which he quickly became the first elected secretary. As he became better acquainted with the students, he was elected as president of the association. While he was president, Pridi Phanomyong would somewhat openly discuss his democratic politics, which connected him to other Thai students with similar viewpoints. After a few years, Pridi had carefully gathered a few close friends and partners that he trusted, and he would often host and attend secretive meetings with them, where they would discuss revolutionary plans for their return to their home country. Through Prayoon Pamornmontri, who was one of the first people Pridi shared his revolutionary plans with and who was also the main recruiter for the revolutionary group, Pridi was connected with Plaek Khittasangkha (Phibun).

Although a revolution was still mostly wishful thinking, Pridi Phanomyong, Prayoon Pamornmontri, and Plaek Khittasangkha yearned for a way to take down the absolute monarchy, creating the People's Party in 1927. Over the subsequent years, Prayoon would continue to recruit fellow Thai students with similar democratic ideologies, and they would go on to play important roles in the Thai revolution of 1932, including Tua Laphanukrom, Nab Phaholyothin,

Lieutenant Luang Sinthu Songgramchai, Phraya Phahon Phayuhasena, Phraya Song Suradej, Phra Prasas Pitthayayudh, and Phraya Ritthi Akaney. Many of these new additions to the revolutionary movement had relatively high-ranking positions in the Siamese military, which would help to provide the movement with necessary military troops, equipment, and planning to eventually overthrow the nation's absolute monarchy.

Although the leaders of the Khana Ratsadon (the People's Party) were plotting revolution for the Kingdom of Siam while in France, their dissatisfaction was similarly shared amongst the people who still remained in the country. While talented students and promising military leaders were sent to study abroad, the younger generation of officials within Thailand who had studied at the newly opened Chulalongkorn University was also gaining expertise and discussing the inefficiency of the nation's political system. This should come as no surprise, considering the dissatisfaction in the Kingdom of Siam within the middle and working classes had been growing ever since King Rama VI's reign. This would mean that the monarchy's power was gradually diminishing, and as a monarchy loses favor with its people, they lose leverage and power since they need to avoid creating more discontentment, as that would lead to revolutions and rebellions.

The royal government's public opinion was not helped by the serious fiscal issues the kingdom was facing at the beginning of the 20th century due to King Rama VI's extravagance and the ramifications of the global Great Depression. These financial difficulties would lead to many cuts within the ministries, which would upset not only the laid-off officials and their families but also the general population. Following the layoffs, Rama VII was forced to make extensive changes in the running of the government to account for the loss of so many high-ranked officials. These changes were not positively received, as the population felt important governmental ministries were not being adequately run.

Another factor that added to the population's distaste for the nation's monarchist government was the shady way decisions were made. Although the government wasn't doing anything necessarily worse than in a democratic political system, the royal family would deliberately keep many actions and decisions secret from the population, who wouldn't find out about even the most extreme changes until they were already put into action. Since the government kept all decisions hidden from the population, newspapers and reporters often printed misinformation based on rumors, although many papers would choose not to print gossip-based news at all since any misrepresentations of the rulers' decisions could end their careers.

Overall, the population was dissatisfied with the absolute monarchist government that had been ruling the Kingdom of Siam since its creation as a nation. However, though the entire population was in favor of political reforms and was leaning more and more toward democratic ideals, it would be the younger Thai students who led the revolution. Toward the end of the 1920s, the members of the newly founded People's Party, who had done all of their plotting abroad, began returning home. Once Pridi Phanomyong, Plaek Khittasangkha, and their revolutionary peers had returned to the Kingdom of Siam, they began building up their forces and somewhat secretly promoting their cause. They gathered fellow democratic Thai students and scholars, both those who had remained in Thailand and those who, like them, had studied abroad. Along with students, they also assembled government and military officials, some of whom had been laid off throughout King Rama VII's reign and some of whom were still in office.

Although the members of the People's Party (known in the Kingdom of Siam as the "Promoters") had spent many years secretly plotting a revolution, it was not until they returned home to Thailand that they began putting their plan into action. Phibun (Plaek Khittasangkha) and fellow revolutionary military officials planned the coup, attempting to avoid violence at all costs. At the same time, Pridi Phanomyong and other People's Party members created a detailed political plan that they hoped to institute if the coup went as planned. The political plan consisted of reforms to the people's liberties, equalities, and educational opportunities, as well as the nation's security, finances, and independence.

On June 24th, 1932, with the Khana Ratsadon, or People's Party, leading as the heart of the movement, a fairly small group of students, military officials, non-royal employed and unemployed government officials, and civilians took to the streets to stage a coup d'état. Catching the monarchical government completely off guard, the Bangkok district, which contained the government buildings, ministries, and palaces, were flooded with people, tanks, and armored cars. The revolutionary group captured, arrested, and imprisoned surprised government officials, many of whom were still in their pajamas. While they were arresting these officials, other members of the People's Party handed out flyers to confused citizens with the revolutionary group's manifesto. The manifesto described how poorly the civilians had been treated by the monarchy, with the flyers saying the government treated people as slaves and as animals. It compared the life of civilians, who had to work their lives away to have enough money to live, with the privilege of the royal family and government officials, who could sleep and eat without worry. The manifesto also detailed how Thailand had one of the worst, if not the worst, government besides the Russians and the Germans and how any other country would have already overthrown their government had it been comparable to that of the Kingdom of Siam.

While the People's Party were staging their rebellion in Bangkok, King Rama VII was golfing at a coastal resort a few hours by train from the city. Ironically, the palace he was staying at, which is a summer residence in Hua Hin for the royal family that had been built for King Rama VII only six years before, is named Klai Kangwon, which directly translates to "far from worry." After contacting both his advisors from within the Kingdom of Siam and his foreign advisors from neighboring and Western countries, King Rama VII realized the monarchy did not stand a chance, as they were unprepared and in the minority. To prevent bloodshed, King Rama VII was essentially forced to capitulate and accept the People's Party's constitution and demands. The People's Party had succeeded in ending the absolute monarchy that had existed in Siam since its creation, and according to the requests of the revolutionary group, the royal family was forced to cede their power to the people of Thailand. Although it took many years of plotting, the People's Party managed to carry out a successful, bloodless coup d'état in only a few hours, leading to the institution of a constitutional regime.

Subsequent Events and Effects of the Thai Revolution of 1932

With the growing dissatisfaction in Thailand during the reigns of the last two absolute monarchist kings, a rebellion was bound to happen at some point, as we can see in the aborted rebellion against King Rama VI in 1912 that had been planned by members of the military. That being said, although the majority of people shared their disgust with the royal government, most people did not agree with the People's Party's revolution.

Although the revolution is often looked at in a positive way, especially at the time by non-Thai scholars who didn't yet know how history would play out, the People's Party's coup was not well taken by much of the country. Many civilians, especially those outside of Bangkok who felt a similar discontent with the government, had nothing to do with the revolution at all and felt the rebellion was just a movement that represented the wants of a small group of students, military and government officials, and Bangkok civilians. To them, this revolution was not what the Kingdom of Siam's population as a whole wanted. Considering the fact that the revolution lacked the country's support, the initial success of the People's Party's movement was short-lived.

On June 26th, 1932, less than two days after the Thai revolution of 1932, the People's Party apologized to the ling and the royal family for the radical and offensive manifesto and requested their help. Despite the Khana Ratsadon's (People's Party) promises of democratic change, King Rama VII and his royal family continued to share power with the newly appointed government in a constitutional monarchist system. This constitutional system, with both the new governing powers and the king running the nation together, continued for the next fifteen years, with the royal family's power gradually diminishing throughout that period.

Chapter 8 – The Constitutional Monarchy and Military Dictatorships (1932–1945)

The People's Party's First Decisions and the Constitutional Monarchy

Similar to the revolution itself, which was incredibly well planned and unbelievably successful, with essentially no issues at all despite all that could have gone wrong, the People's Party had been meticulously planning out many aspects of their future government practices. However, unlike the revolution, their well-thought-out new political system did not go as planned.

In 1932, following the coup, Pridi Phanomyong helped to craft the constitution that would detail the king and his role in the government and how the power would be gradually transferred to a new democratic governing order. The transference of power was supposed to occur in three stages. First, the People's Party would appoint seventy government representatives, made up of both members of the People's Party and, in a democratic fashion, new non-royal officials who played no part in the revolution at all. This way, the People's Party would be staying true to their democratic goals without flooding the government with completely new, untrained people. The government would still be made up of many of the king's government officials, who had the experience necessary to train the new representatives to ensure the transition of power went smoothly.

In the second stage, the People's Party would continue to gradually rule out the king's men from governmental positions unless they were chosen by the people to remain. Finally, during the third period, the power would be completely transferred, and the political system would be completely democratic. The plan was that once the government had reached the third stage of the transition plan, all government officials would be democratically elected by the population and not appointed directly by any higher force, so neither the king nor the People's Party would have the power to decide officials; it would instead be up to the regular civilians.

Their goal was for the nation to reach the final government form once at least 50 percent of the population had a primary education, which was a readily growing number due to the efforts of King Rama V and the laws made by King Rama VI. That being said, if half the population had still not completed their primary education within ten years of the creation of the constitution, which was finalized on December 10th, 1932, the final stage would begin regardless.

During these ten years, the People's Party promised to help improve the nation's economy and help send more Thais to receive a post-secondary education. The push for education would come as no surprise since the People's Party was made up almost entirely of university-educated scholars, intellectuals, and military officials. The party set up the University of Moral and Political Science, which would attempt to make higher education more common and widespread throughout the nation. Considering the People's Party inherited a post-Great Depression Thailand, they had no choice but to reform the government's economic policies to help remedy the country's fiscal issues. Some economic changes that the People's Party promised following the revolution and delivered on were putting an end to the overcharging of interest and the confiscation of agriculturalists' properties.

The members of the People's Party were well aware that their new power would require them to tackle some of the financial issues the kingdom had been facing over the past few decades. At the beginning of 1933, not even a year after the Thai revolution of 1932, Pridi wrote an economic plan that he announced to the government, which, at this point, was still dominated by the king's chosen officials. His plan was aggressive, radical, and significantly more democratic and socialist than the old, more conservative government officials were willing to accept. It was even too extreme for the new officials to put into place. The almost communist-leaning economic plan, which detailed Pridi's goals of nationalizing all industrial and commercial assets and enterprises and making all workers into state employees, upset just about everyone.

Pridi Phanomyong's economic plan was so controversial that it was not only rejected immediately with no deliberation, but it also earned him the reputation of a somewhat deranged communist, a reputation that would follow him for the rest of his life. The radical economic plan upset so many people that Pridi was temporarily exiled, and to avoid further complications, the king temporarily suspended the newly formed National Assembly. Although King Rama VII suspended the National Assembly in order to prevent any more governmental controversies that may turn off more royalists, the People's Party realized that this meant their own power would be temporarily limited. The radical plan also led to the removal of the first prime minister of Thailand, Phraya Manopakorn Nititada, who was elected by the People's Party directly after the revolution, meaning he didn't hold his office for even a full year.

With the People's Party being so new, they feared that even a temporary suspension of the National Assembly might allow the king and his royal order to regain their power over the government. To prevent any attempts to steal back control of the nation, the People's

Party's military leaders forced King Rama VII to revive the National Assembly. Less than a year after the first coup, a new coup to reconstitute the National Assembly took place. It was led by Luang Phibunsongkhram (Phibun). While in the process of reviving the National Assembly, Phibun installed a longtime member of the People's Party, Phraya Phahon Phayuhasena, as the second prime minister of Siam.

Between the People's Party's democratic ideologies, Pridi Phanomyong's socialist economic plan, and the military leaders forcing the reconstitution of the National Assembly, the royalists, especially the older and more conservative ones, were not pleased with the new government. The royalists demonstrated their discontent in a countercoup rebellion that took place over the course of a few tense days in October of 1933. Although King Rama VII had no involvement in the rebellion, it was led by his cousin, Prince Boworadet. In this battle, Lieutenant Colonel Phibun's military intelligence and prowess would once again shine, as he led his troops and suppressed the countercoup within only three days of intense fighting. Though King Rama VII had absolutely no involvement or connection to the royalist rebellion in 1933, it was at this point that he felt his position was no longer personally maintainable. A few months after the attempted countercoup, King Rama VII left the country and moved to England, and just over a year after that, he abdicated his role as king. Although Siam was no longer a nation led by a monarch, Prince Ananda Mahidol, who would become King Rama VIII, was named as the successor to the throne, but seeing as the prince was only nine at the time and studying abroad in Switzerland, a regency council would act in his place until he returned.

Phibunsongkhram (Phibun) was already considered to be an impressive military leader following the Thai revolution of 1932, but it took resisting the royalist rebellion of 1933 for him to come into public prominence. Although neither the previous royalist government nor the People's Party, or even the population for that matter, was fully aware of it at the time, Siam was slowly being controlled by its military. Led by Lieutenant Colonel Phibun, as well as other well-trained military officers, the military would continue to strengthen and gain power. Between the years of 1933 and 1938, the military grew and gained experience, even though it was only fighting internally within its own nation. In fact, the new and improved military run by the People's Party would not actually have the chance to face an external force or threat of any kind until 1941.

Only a few years after the Thai revolution of 1932, some obvious cracks were forming in the People's Party. The government was essentially split into three different groups, with the first being the royalists made up of the king's remaining family and conservative elitist royally-appointed officials. The second group was represented by the non-military members of the People's Party and the elected civilian government officials. The final group within the government was the military, led by extreme members of the People's Party and other well-disciplined military generals. The three rivaling factions would continue to battle for the upper hand in the subsequent years following the original revolution of 1932. Ultimately, through a series of military rebellions and coups that plagued the nation in the 1930s, the military wing would unsurprisingly triumph over the other two governmental factions. This would eventually lead to the military dictatorship that would control the country of Thailand for years to come.

Pridi Phanomyong returned to his home country in 1934, after just over a year of exile abroad. Upon returning to Siam, he founded the nation's second university, the aforementioned University of Moral and Political Science, also known as Thammasat University. By opening the university, Pridi was able to deliver on one of his core beliefs and promises at the beginning of his campaign, which was that higher education should be accessible to all who wanted it, not only those of the royal family. The same year he returned, he was elected as the minister of the interior, which would give him responsibility for appointing the governors of the provinces of Thailand, internal security, local administration, citizenship, and other facets of internal affairs. Not long after becoming the minister of the interior, he was appointed as the minister of foreign affairs. During his time holding this position, Pridi attempted to renegotiate all of the unfair treaties between Thailand and foreign, mostly European, countries. He would help to put an end to the remaining foreign countries' extraterritorial rights in Siam and limit the import taxes that Western countries had put in place to take advantage of Siam.

The Beginning of the Military Dictatorship in Thailand

Although Pridi Phanomyong represented the civilian wing of the government, it was essentially upon his return that the government's military faction began gaining power. In 1934, following Phibun's impressive triumphs over the royalists in their attempted countercoup, he became the country's minister of defense. Subsequent to his rise in rank, he would dedicate himself to strengthening the nation's army. Much like King Rama VI or King Rama VII, who also studied abroad, Phibun was inspired by Western governments and ideologies. Unlike the previous kings who seemed to take most of their inspiration from their time studying in Britain, Phibun was enamored and impressed with the Italian military fascist movement led by Benito Mussolini, which was occurring while Phibun had been in Europe. He realized the potential and power of nationalism and saw the effects of government-issued propaganda. On top of working to strengthen the nation's troops, he attempted to popularize military and nationalistic values based on those he had come to appreciate in Italy. He would push Italian propaganda films and started presenting himself as a hero to the Thai people. Though Pridi Phanomyong marked the beginning of many new privileges for the citizens of Siam, at the same time, the government was shifting toward a fascist regime that not only slowed the promised democratic changes down but also took away some of the civilians' rights and equalities.

Phibun was certainly aided throughout his time as minister of defense due to the fact that his backer, Phraya Phahon Phayuhasena, had been the prime minister of Siam. However, after being appointed as the second prime minister in 1933 following the Thai revolution of 1932, Phraya Phahon was involved in a scandal concerning shady real estate deals. After five years as the prime minister of Siam, Phraya Phahon was forced to retire, and the country held its first-ever election in 1937.

The 1937 election in Thailand would elect around half of the seats in the National Assembly. Pridi Phanomyong would be elected as the minister of finance, but more importantly, Phibun would be chosen as the new prime minister of Siam, becoming the country's first elected prime minister. He would assume the position in December of 1938 and began imposing his ultranationalistic beliefs on the population almost immediately. Although he was democratically elected, upon assuming the position of prime minister, the government, under his guidance, began tilting toward complete military fascism. Phibun essentially became the unofficial dictator of Siam. To assert his power, Prime Minister Phibunsongkhram arrested his opposition, especially the remaining royalists and members of the royal family who had long challenged his opinions. By doing so, Phibun was quite quickly dominating the civilians in office and, in many ways, moving away from the People's Party's initial plans of democracy and returning to a government that shared many similarities with absolute kingship.

Since Prime Minister Phibunsongkhram quite openly opposed the Chinese, who had inhabited Siam for centuries at this point, similar to beliefs held by many fascist dictators when it comes to people of other nationalities, the non-Thai civilians clashed with his ultranationalistic views. Phibun very quickly rolled out many policies that were intended to curb the Chinese civilians' success in the country. He tried his best to restrict Chinese education and limited the usage of Mandarin in Chinese schools. Phibun pushed to reduce Chinese immigration to Siam, and in 1939, he officially changed the name of the country from Siam to Thailand. This change was to rid the country of its name that had been assigned by foreigners and to push his anti-Chinese rhetoric that Thailand was the land for the Thai. Ironically enough, "Thai," a name given to the civilians of the Kingdom of Siam in 1238 upon their liberation of the controlling Khmer Empire, translates to "free." Although the Thai and the country of Thailand had been freed from oppressive forces many times throughout history, the name was changed in a period where civilians had their freedoms revoked.

While the democratic Pridi Phanomyong was acting as the country's minister of finance, working on revamping the taxation system to remove unfair taxes not based upon earnings, Phibun was using taxes to reduce Chinese economic power. The Chinese, who had arrived in Thailand centuries before for economic opportunities, had quite successful and prosperous businesses, which Phibun denounced, claiming they were trying to take opportunities away from the native Thais. He offered Thai-owned businesses subsidies and pushed civilians to support them rather than Chinese ones. All of these actions would lead officials with opposing views, especially those of Chinese heritage, to compare the Phibunsongkhram movement against the Chinese to what was occurring to the Jewish population in Germany around the same time (this was just prior to World War II).

While promoting anti-Chinese beliefs, Phibun felt it was necessary that the Thais developed their own culture that was distinct from the Chinese. Although the Thais had established a uniquely rich culture of their own, Phibun felt it had too many close ties with Chinese culture, which had helped to shape it. In 1939, Phibun issued a new national anthem, which, similar to any national anthem, pushes patriotism and ultranationalism. The anthem's lyrics detail the Thai civilians' responsibility and willingness to fight for their nation. Although the song quite fairly speaks of Thai independence, an understanding of the anti-Chinese events surrounding the inception of the song gives another meaning to lyrics such as "every inch of Thailand belongs to the Thais."

Similar to the kings who had preceded him, who had similarly studied in Europe before their reign, Phibun pushed his nationalistic beliefs by introducing new Western practices, which he believed would be necessary to modernize the country. Prime Minister Phibunsongkhram imposed decrees that encouraged the civilians to wear more Western-style fashions, an act that King Rama VI had tried to pass a few decades before and was faced with great adversity for doing so. Phibun succeeded where King Rama VI had failed, though, and prohibited betel chewing and made opium illegal. All those addicted to the substance were prosecuted and jailed. In 1940, he changed the traditional celebration of New Year's from April to the Western month of celebration in January, although the decree didn't take. Today, Thais celebrate both dates and have kept the April New Year's as their traditional celebration.

Thailand during World War II (1939–1945)

While pushing for fascist, Western-style, ultra-Thai nationalism, and anti-Chinese policies internally, World War II was beginning externally. Prime Minister Phibunsongkhram took advantage of France's misfortune in 1940 at the start of World War II and provoked a war with French Indochina to attempt to regain the land that had previously belonged to Thailand. The war waged between 1940 and 1941, but seeing as France was preoccupied in their home country, they were unable to resist Phibun's irredentist claims. Thailand regained their lost territory in Cambodia and Laos with the help of Japanese forces, which helped to form an alliance between the two countries.

As Phibun slowly shifted from being the prime minister to the country's military dictator, his appreciation for Japanese military practices grew. Throughout his reign, he was quite openly pro-Japanese, and an alliance had been forged between the two countries when Japan supported Phibun's claim to lost lands in Cambodia and

Laos. At the start of World War II, Japan's own nationalistic views led it to join Germany, and along with Italy, the three countries formed the Axis Powers. Following Japan's attack on Pearl Harbor in the United States, which succeeded since no one saw it coming, Japan plotted a similar surprise attack in 1941 on British Singapore. To be able to reach Singapore unannounced, Japan planned to travel through Thailand, as an attack wouldn't be expected to come from that direction. In 1941, with the intention of surprising Singapore, Japanese troops entered Thailand, and since the two countries had previously forged an alliance, Japan requested the Thai government for the right of passage. The Thai government, not wanting to facilitate an attack on their Western allies, attempted to resist the Japanese troops. However, after only a brief period of battling, Phibun's pro-Japanese views and his realizations that resistance would probably only lead to the partial destruction of Thailand led him to sign a treaty of alliance with Japan, which would allow their new ally to peacefully cross through Thailand.

Just before and during World War II, the once-democratic People's Party had transitioned into a fully fascist military dictatorship led by elected Prime Minister Phibunsongkhram. This, of course, upset almost all of the original civilian members of the People's Party, including Pridi Phanomyong, Phibun's counterpart in the Thai revolution of 1932. Throughout the Phibun dictatorship, many of the civilians holding governmental positions were released of their duties and replaced with those who backed Phibun's fascist views. In 1941, following Phibun's signing of the treaty with Japan, which only strengthened the dictatorship's fascist rule, Pridi Phanomyong resigned as the minister of finance; however, whether it was by choice or force is still unknown. Pridi was assigned the role of regent in place of King Ananda Mahidol (King Rama VIII), who was not only quite young still but also stuck in Europe during World War II.

Following Thailand's treaty with Japan, Phibun and his government declared war on the Western countries that opposed Japan, specifically the United States and Great Britain, at the beginning of 1942. Thailand's signing of the treaty with Japan, Phibun's pro-fascist government, and the country's declaration of war on the United States and Britain would unravel many of the alliances that had been made between Thailand and the Western countries over the previous years and alienate Thailand from the West for years to come.

Considering the fact that the treaty signed between Japan and Thailand was formed not due to the alliance the two countries had built over the years but rather created to end a battle caused by a Japanese invasion, it is not surprising that the Japanese took advantage of their new privileges. Following the treaty, Thailand's government was increasingly undermined by the Japanese occupation, which caused both the Thai economy and population to suffer. The public began to lose trust in Phibun's government, which led to the creation of numerous resistance groups. Pridi Phanomyong, who was by this point anti-Japanese and completely against Phibun's government, led the Free Thai (*Seri Thai*) movement, a resistance group created to rid the country of the Japanese occupation. The Free Thai organization connected with resistance groups based in the West, mainly in the United States, which helped to revitalize Thailand's foreign relations in the future. Pridi Phanomyong, operating within the Thai resistance groups under the codename Ruth, organized rebellions against the Japanese and the Thai government. By 1944, when it became increasingly obvious that the Axis was not going to win, Phibun's government collapsed, and he was forced to resign in July of 1944. A civilian government, led unofficially by Pridi and headed officially by Khuang Aphaiwong, replaced Phibun's government. World War II officially ended on September 2nd, 1945.

Chapter 9 – Power Struggles in Thailand Post World War II (1945–1973)

Democratic Rule Post Phibunsongkhram's First Military Dictatorship

In 1944, Phibunsongkhram (Phibun) was forced to resign as the prime minister of Thailand, and he was replaced on July 31st by Khuang Aphaiwong. Khuang Aphaiwong was the son of a Thai governor, and like many children of government officials, he had gone on to study in the West. Khuang Aphaiwong pursued post-secondary education in engineering in France, and it was there that he made connections to Phibunsongkhram and Pridi Phanomyong. He was even one of the founding members of the People's Party. Although Khuang Aphaiwong would only hold the position of prime minister for a few months following the fall of Phibun's military rule, he would subsequently hold the position again two more times for similarly short periods over the next few years.

Khuang Aphaiwong's first period in office as acting prime minister of Thailand was unusual since he found himself wedged between the democratic civilians of the People's Party, now the Free Thai, and the military leaders that he had openly helped during the war (although he did not really have much choice in the matter if he wanted to keep his job). Though Khuang Aphaiwong was technically the prime minister, many of the decisions made by the government toward the end of and subsequent to World War II were actually made by Pridi Phanomyong, who was working behind the scenes.

In 1945, the last year of World War II, Thailand helped the Allies in every way possible. Pridi Phanomyong retracted Thailand's previous declaration of war against the United States and Britain and allowed the Allies free access in Bangkok. Very quickly after replacing Phibun, Pridi Phanomyong and Khuang Aphaiwong terminated the treaty the previous military dictator had signed with Japan, officially ending their alliance. These swift changes would help remedy Thailand's international reputation and prevent potential military threats from the west from occurring. This likely would have taken place had the government waited any longer. Under its new democratic rule, Thailand returned the territories in Laos and Cambodia that had been taken from France during World War II. Due to all of the reparations made toward the end of World War II, Thailand's global reputation was rectified, and the country was admitted to the United Nations in 1946. Directly following the end of the war, King Ananda Mahidol (King Rama VIII) was able to return from Europe, and Pridi Phanomyong was reassigned as a senior statesman, seeing as he was no longer needed as regent.

Despite the collapse of the military dictatorship bringing about a period of democracy, the government was far from secure. Just as they had at the beginning of the 1930s when the People's Party first took control of the government, many cracks appeared in the newly reigning democratic party. Although Khuang Aphaiwong and Pridi Phanomyong had helped to advance Thailand subsequent to the collapse of Phibun's reign, they were not united and began to fall out around the time World War II ended. Due to these instabilities, Khuang Aphaiwong was replaced by Thawi Bunyaket after only a year in office. Thawi would be replaced not even two months later by Seni

Pramoj. Seni had been the original choice, but he wasn't available when Khuang stepped down. This would help to stabilize the party for a short period, but the party would never be truly united during their reign, which would eventually lead to their downfall.

In September of 1945, Seni Pramoj assumed the position of prime minister of Thailand. This would be Seni Pramoj's first stint as prime minister, a position he would hold four separate times over the course of the next few decades, for a combined total of only just about a year. Seni Pramoj was one of many living great-grandsons of King Rama II, and as with almost all of the younger generations of royal family members, he received a foreign education in the West. Seni attended Trent College, which is an English boarding school, and like King Rama VI, he went on to study at the prestigious Oxford University. At Oxford, Seni studied law, and after passing his bar exams, he returned to Bangkok to work as a junior judge. Although Seni was of royal blood, he was never truly opposed to the People's Party's coup in 1932, likely due to his education abroad. That being said, he was not necessarily fond of the members of the People's Party or how they ran the country. There are many rumors surrounding Seni Pramoj's opinions since his views on issues seemed to have greatly changed many times during World War II. At first, Seni publicly and firmly supported Phibun's government, but he seemed to completely reverse his opinions once the government signed the treaty with Japan. Despite his frequently varying opinions, Seni Pramoj became a symbol of the Thai resistance, which would aid him in being chosen as the prime minister at the end of World War II.

When Seni Pramoj was prime minister, he was, to his dismay, controlled by Pridi Phanomyong, just as Khuang Aphaiwong had been. Although the democratic government under Seni flourished, this period led to larger cracks in the People's Party and amongst the democrats in the country. Toward the end of Seni Pramoj's short term as prime minister, the country was suffering due to post-war alliances and reparations made with Western countries. To rid the air of war that remained between Thailand and Britain post World War II, Seni and his government signed a peace treaty in January of 1946, which Britain would only sign if Thailand agreed to post-war reparations, including cripplingly large amounts of rice. These post-war alliances led to serious financial difficulties, which led to the population's discontentment with Seni Pramoj's government. As the population's dissatisfaction grew, Seni left his post as prime minister, which was somewhat unjust since many of the upsetting decisions were actually made by Pridi Phanomyong. This would only aid to further the cracks in the democratic movements in Thailand and forge a rivalry of sorts between Seni Pramoj and Pridi Phanomyong. Seni was replaced by Khuang Aphaiwong, who took the position once again under his unofficially founded Democrat Party, which would be officially founded in April of 1946. This time around, Khuang assumed the position for less than three months.

Khuang Aphaiwong was prime minister for a little over fifty days, but seeing as his party was not properly established, he resigned on March 24th, 1946, following a vote of no-confidence. Khuang Aphaiwong would go on to formally establish the Democrat Party on April 6th, 1946, which would act as a rivaling democratic party to the People's Party and make it clear that the country's democratic forces had separated. Thailand's Democrat Party would illustrate the cracks that had formed in the People's Party, as Khuang Aphaiwong would be joined by Seni Pramoj since they both shared a distaste for Pridi Phanomyong, who had controlled them from behind the scenes during their respective periods as prime minister. The party would attract other democratic-leaning royalists, including Seni Pramoj's brother, Kukrit Pramoj, and members of the Thai resistance who had lost trust in the People's Party and specifically in Pridi Phanomyong.

Although every leader since 1932 had technically been democratically elected, it wasn't until 1946 that the country held its first popular election. This would mean that when Pridi Phanomyong was elected as prime minister in March of 1946, he was the first-ever prime minister elected fully by the people. Similar to when Pridi Phanomyong's People's Party took power in 1932, in 1946, Pridi came prepared to make some significant changes to the country without any delay. He very quickly passed a new constitution that would help to protect civilians' labor rights, return democratic power to the population, and hopefully reduce the military's power in Thailand's government once and for all. Pridi Phanomyong, who had been essentially running the government from behind the scenes since 1944, had finally earned his position as prime minister and intended to make the radical reforms he felt were necessary to restore Thailand, which had been rocked by both World War II and Phibun's abusive military dictatorship, which stripped the citizens of many of their liberties.

Though Pridi Phanomyong made initial progress at the start of his reign, making it seem like Thailand would finally be able to recover from the damages they had experienced over the past few decades, the peace was short-lived. On June 9th, 1946, twenty-year-old King Ananda Mahidol (King Rama VIII), who had only returned to his home country six months prior, was found dead. The young king was found in his bed in the royal palace, with the cause of death a gunshot wound. King Ananda Mahidol's death left just about everyone in confusion. No one was sure if it was an accident, a murder, or even suicide. Even the king's brother Bhumibol, who would become King Rama IX, claimed that it was certainly not a suicide or an accident, but he was still unsure as to what had happened. Seeing as Pridi Phanomyong's officials were never able to solve the investigation, the death was ruled as an accident, although almost no one in Thailand felt the case was closed.

The military leaders from Phibun's rule and the Democrat Party did not agree on much, but in some way, they unknowingly banded together in their mutual suspicion, or at least mutual blame, of Pridi Phanomyong, implicating him as the mastermind behind the death of the young King Ananda Mahidol. Throughout 1946, both the

Democrat Party and the fallen military government spread their beliefs of the prime minister's involvement in King Ananda Mahidol's sudden death. The Democrat Party, being a more trusted organization at this point, was responsible for much of the propaganda. Trusted members of parliament from the Democrat Party would claim that Pridi Phanomyong had been the architect behind the king's death and that his death was truly an assassination. No matter what one believed, almost no one believed a proper investigation had been completed by the government or police at the time of the king's death. Pridi Phanomyong's case was not helped by the fact that his government had released very little information about the case, keeping most of the facts hidden from the public.

Whether Pridi Phanomyong was truly involved in the death of King Ananda Mahidol does not matter. In the end, the population lost trust in Pridi and his government, and the controversies surrounding his possible assassination attempt would weaken his government to the point of no return. On August 21st, 1946, after less than barely five months as prime minister, Pridi Phanomyong resigned. Pridi would publicly announce that he resigned due to his poor health, although it is more likely that he was forced by his party to do so. After being one of the leading members of the Thai revolution of 1932, Pridi Phanomyong would spend only a few years subsequent to his return from exile and the two years following World War II with any sort of power in the country. Following Pridi Phanomyong's resignation as prime minister, the position would be filled by various democratic leaders, including Khuang Aphaiwong, Seni Pramoj, and Kukrit Pramoj, who would each hold the office for short periods of time without the previous stability or security. Following King Ananda Mahidol's death, the throne would be succeeded by his nineteen-year-old brother Bhumibol Adulyadej, who became known as King Rama IX and would remain abroad until 1951. He would go on to become the longest-reigning monarch of

Thailand and is, as of now, the second-longest reigning monarch of all time.

Pridi Phanomyong fled from Thailand once and for all in 1947. He moved to China and stayed there until 1970, when he then left Asia to return to France, the country that had inspired him to lead the revolutionary movement and push for democracy in Thailand in the first place. From both China and France, Pridi Phanomyong would speak out about his criticisms of the subsequent fascist Thailand governments that would rule throughout the rest of Pridi's life. From fleeing Thailand until his death, Pridi was never able to see true democracy in his home country, nor was he ever allowed to return. Seeing as no one, foreigners included, were allowed to discuss or even write about King Ananda Mahidol's tragic death, up to Pridi Phanomyong's death in 1983, he was regarded by most as a villain, as they saw him as being the one responsible for the assassination of King Ananda. It would not be until the end of the 20th century, when people were allowed to speak of the events surrounding King Ananda's death, that Pridi would be cleared of the suspicions clouding his name and recognized as an important revolutionary figure in Thailand's history. Years later, many scholars have made the case that it is actually more likely that Phibunsongkhram (Phibun) and his allies were responsible for the young king's death, especially considering how much the king's death worked in the military wing's favor. However, it is impossible to know what actually happened, as there are numerous theories regarding the young king's death.

Reinstatement of the Military Dictatorship with Phibunsongkhram as the Prime Minister

The fact that the population had turned against the democratic civilian-run government worked out perfectly for Phibun's military faction. Although Thailand's civilians, as well as foreign countries, had not necessarily gotten over Phibun's alliance with the Japanese and aggressive nationalism, they were even more disappointed with Pridi Phanomyong and his supporters. The intelligent yet manipulative

Phibun and his military government played on the population's resentment of the democratic government's decisions after World War II. The military faction knew that the public resented the democratic-approved war reparations that had caused so much economic suffering in the years following the war. Although the post-war reparations were only necessary due to Phibun's decision to join the Japanese in fighting the Western Allies in World War II, the population was so dissatisfied with the crippling reparations that they turned their blame to the democratic government instead. Phibun's reputation amongst the civilians and foreign countries was also aided by the fact that he was always very openly anti-communist. His staunch anti-communism was especially sought after in the 20th century, as communism was growing in Thailand's neighboring countries. This meant that he earned the respect and support from other anti-communist leaders and countries, such as the United States.

In November of 1947, the military, led by Phibun and some other military generals who had backed Phibun during his military government, namely Phin Choonhavan, staged a coup, seizing the democratic civilian government. During the coup, Phibun threatened all those who still backed Pridi Phanomyong; it was during this coup that Pridi narrowly escaped Thailand, never to return to his home country.

Although Phibun and his military party had regained popularity in the country, the military faction was well aware that the population was not quite ready for them to take control of the government again. Thawal Thamrongnavaswadhi was the prime minister at the time of the military coup of 1937, and he still quietly supported Pridi Phanomyong. In their efforts to not anger the civilians while still removing or arresting all those who continued to support Pridi Phanomyong, the military faction named the democratic Khuang Abhaiwongse as interim prime minister until a new election could be held.

In January 1948, around two months after the military coup, the government held a general election, and although the military leaders did well, the military faction chose to keep Khuang Abhaiwongse as the prime minister to avoid any countercoups from the democratic civilians. Khuang Abhaiwongse continued being prime minister, although his power was limited by the military faction. Within a few months, the military powers were dissatisfied with Khuang's overly democratic practices, and in April of 1948, Khuang Abhaiwongse would be forced to resign.

Similar to the military reign preceding and during World War II, Phibun played a major role in leading the military movement. However, the coup of 1947 differs with that of the military reign, as this time around, Phibun shared his political power with two generals: General Phao Siyanon and General Sarit Thanarat. Both of these men had helped Phibun overthrow the People's Party's government in 1947. Over the next few years, during which military power continued to grow, General Phao Siyanon and General Sarit Thanarat would gain power over Phibun, and they would eventually depose him altogether a decade after reclaiming power over Thailand.

In 1948, Phibun would reassume the position of prime minister, which he would keep until 1957. Although he was gradually becoming less powerful than his younger counterparts, a rivalry between General Phao Siyanon and General Sarit Thanarat prevented either one from replacing Phibun. Throughout his term as prime minister, Phibun would share much of his power and make many of his decisions with the help of Phao Siyanon and Sarit Thanarat.

Akin to Phibun's reign as prime minister in the 1930s and early 1940s, Phibun's government was not exactly a true military dictatorship. Although it resembles one, with many of its policies being inspired by fascist governments, a true military dictatorship was not put in place until the power was taken away from Phibun in 1957. That being said, Phibun and his associates led Thailand with an iron fist and reintroduced many extreme, ultranationalist, and freedom-revoking practices, ones that Phibun had instituted during his first period as prime minister. To placate the unrest, a new constitution was formed with the help of the Democrat Party, before Khuang Abhaiwongse and his fellow party members were forced to take their leave. However, not long after, Phibun and his associates reinstituted the 1932 constitution, which would once again limit many of the civilians' rights. In 1946, prior to Phibun assuming the position of prime minister, the nation reverted its name back to Siam to retract some of the extreme nationalism that had led to the change in its name. However, in 1949, Phibun and his colleagues restored the country's name to Thailand, the land of the Thais. Once again, one must notice the irony in this timing, as the country's name also translates to "land of the free." Phibunsongkhram continued his anti-Chinese rhetoric, although this time around, this harassment was celebrated, seeing as the Chinese outside of Thailand were becoming increasingly communist during this time. Phibun reintroduced his Western-leaning beliefs and decrees, many of which were seen as negative, but some, such as the improvement of secondary education, resulted in positive changes for the nation.

Overall, the beginning of Phibun's reign was, unsurprisingly, not overwhelmingly well-received. Over the subsequent years after assuming the post, Phibun and his associates would have to deal with rebellions, coups, and unrest from almost every other governmental faction. Phibun survived rebellions by rival military factions in 1948, 1949, and 1951, though in 1951, Phibun was actually abducted. The military government was able to resist the three coups, and in 1951, following the brief abduction of the prime minister, they revoked the newly written constitution and replaced it with the 1932 constitution, the more restrictive one, instead.

Despite all of Phibun's and his associates' reimposed restrictive practices, the government during this period was and still is celebrated for their anti-communist actions. Immediately after reassuming the position of prime minister, Phibun began fighting the communists both internally within Thailand and externally within Thailand's neighboring countries. The West began realizing the potential of an anti-communist country located so close to the rapidly growing communist countries in Asia. Phibun once again pushed for the suppression of the Chinese inhabitants in Thailand, this time in the name of fighting communism. Thailand aided the English and Malay troops in fighting against communists located in the south of Thailand around the Thailand-Malaysia border.

During the Korean War, which began in 1950, the United States sent money to help support Thailand's military. The government would use this money to send 4,000 Thai troops to help the United Nations fight against the communist Koreans. The United States' financial support would also fortify Thailand's economy, remedying many of the existing financial issues that had been affecting the country since King Rama VI's reign. Thailand would continue to help the United States and the United Nations fight the spread of communism in 1954 during the Cold War when Phibun helped to form SEATO (the Southeast Asia Treaty Organization), which was an anti-communist defense organization. Despite Phibun's results in fighting communism, both the Thai population and his military faction were growing dissatisfied with his use of power.

Considering General Phao Siyanon and General Sarit Thanarat were gradually becoming more powerful than Phibun, it should come as no surprise that he would eventually be replaced by one of them. As Phibun gained the confidence of foreign countries in his fight against communism, he lost the confidence of the population and his government. The middle- and higher-class citizens were becoming increasingly dissatisfied with Phibun's economic results. Although the nation's economic situation would improve due to the money sent by the United States, Phibun's nationalistic economic plan was proving to be unsuccessful. His military colleagues were equally discontent with his reign, and Sarit Thanarat would up being the one to lead the long-awaited coup against Phibun's tiresome reign. The coup, which took place in September of 1957, would successfully overthrow Phibun and force the man who had introduced the military government to Thailand into exile. In time, Sarit Thanarat would become the prime minister, who would introduce a true extreme military dictatorship to the country.

General Sarit Thanarat and his Successors' Military Dictatorships

In September of 1957, Sarit Thanarat was elected as field marshal, and a provisional prime minister named Pote Sarasin was appointed. In December of that year, a parliamentary election was held. On January 1st, 1958, Thanom Kittikachorn was chosen as the new prime minister, but he was overthrown by Sarit Thanarat on October 20th, 1958, due to another military coup, a system of toppling political leaders that had come to plague the country by this point.

Although Sarit Thanarat was even more fascist and extreme than his predecessor Phibun, he was respected by the population. The day after he assumed his position as prime minister, or rather dictator, Sarit Thanarat suspended the constitution, which would be officially replaced on January 28th, 1959. During Sarit Thanarat's term, he sought to clean Thailand up from crime and corruption and improve the country's economic practices and policies.

Sarit Thanarat only held this position of power until his death in 1963, during which time he would greatly reform the nation and help shape it into the country it is today. Almost immediately after overthrowing the previous government, Sarit Thanarat took Thailand's social issues into his own hands. He launched campaigns against corruption in the national police force, worked to lessen organized crime, and put an end to the drug consumption and trade, specifically of opium, in Thailand. In his short reign, he also completely transformed Thailand's education system, which, up to that point, had been seriously lacking in comparison to Western countries, which explains why most Thai intellectuals and royal family members would attend schools in Europe rather than Thailand.

Unlike the other democratic leaders and the military dictator Phibun, Sarit Thanarat sought the approval of the king, which at that time was still King Bhumibol Adulyadej (King Rama IX). By 1960, Sarit helped reestablish the monarchy's influence to a new generation, which had grown up without the monarchy being involved in the government or politics at all.

Sarit Thanarat would completely restructure the nation's economic policies, which were in serious need of an overhaul. Aided by the money Thailand was still receiving from the United States following Phibun's anti-communist practices, Thailand was able to grow its own products and take advantage of its own resources. Sarit Thanarat spent much of his time in office focusing on growing Thailand's domestic product and their foreign investments. Although the money the country was receiving from the United States was intended for the military, with much of it going toward that branch of government, Sarit Thanarat also used the money to construct new highways, establish rural economic development, build more schools, and make electricity more accessible. Similar to his predecessor Phibun, Sarit Thanarat was openly allied with the United States and was staunchly against communism, which was necessary for the country to keep receiving funds from America.

Despite all of the positive changes that Sarit Thanarat made, he oversaw a truly aggressive military dictatorship. Almost immediately after assuming the leadership position, Sarit dissolved the parliament, and after abolishing the constitution, he suspended all the democratic constitutional rights that the population had once again begun to get used to. Sarit Thanarat's authoritarian regime was marked by the limiting of free speech, which included the banning of newspapers and media that did not favor his political party, and the banning of other political parties. Although Sarit Thanarat was popular and achieved much good for the nation during his rule, his reputation became increasingly negative following his death in 1963. Although Sarit Thanarat had greatly opposed Phibun and the police force's corruption, only after his death did the truth come out about the ruler's own corrupt practices, which would haunt his and his successors' reputations.

In 1963, Sarit Thanarat was succeeded by Thanom Kittikachorn, who kept many of his predecessor's practices in place. Thanom Kittikachorn, who was helped by Praphas Charusathian, the Deputy Prime Minister of Thailand, continued to receive funds from the United States Army in exchange for further help against the communist countries. During Thanom Kittikachorn's military dictatorship, the United States military and, by 1969, over 11,000 Thai troops were involved in the war with Vietnam. Similar to their predecessors, Thanom Kittikachorn and Praphas Charusathian would accept American money that helped stimulate the Thai economy. Although this had been occurring for many years, it was only after Sarit Thanarat's death that people were made aware of the corruption surrounding the intake of American money, as these funds only helped to increase the gap between the rich and those beneath the poverty line.

Toward the end of the 1960s, between the dissatisfaction for the government's oppressive authoritarian rule and the obvious corruption occurring with the American money, the people, especially those in the working and middle classes, were displeased with the country's government. It would seem, once again, the rebellions would be in the hands of students. A revolution movement, led by students who had received foreign education and picked up democratic ideals in Europe, began holding public demonstrations to oppose the fascist government. The nation's discontent would continue to escalate between the end of the 1960s and the start of the 1970s until that fateful day of October 14th, 1973.

Chapter 10 – The Struggle for Democracy in Modern Thailand (1973–2020)

The 1973 Thai Popular Uprising

By the beginning of the 1970s, Thailand had endured twenty-five years of interrupted, strict military dictatorship rule under Phibunsongkhram (Phibun), Sarit Thanarat, Thanom Kittikachorn, and Praphas Charusathian. Similar to the years that led up to the Thai revolution of 1932, which overthrew the absolute monarchy, discontentment was growing amongst the population, who were tired of autocratic rule. These frustrations would be demonstrated through various student-led protests throughout the 1960s and the beginning of the 1970s. Thailand's dictator, Thanom Kittikachorn, just as King Rama VII had been before he was ousted, was well aware of the population's growing dissatisfaction. To try and placate the civilians, Thanom introduced some insignificant democratic reforms and promised to bring the country back toward a democratic government once communism, both internally and in neighboring countries, was triumphed. In 1971, Thanom Kittikachorn would remove the minor democratic changes he had made and reimpose the military rule, and in 1972, a new constitution was created that would strip the population of more freedoms than ever before.

In 1972, students from different universities in Thailand formed the National Student Center of Thailand (NSCT), with Thirayuth Boonmee, an engineering student, as the face of the movement. Throughout 1972 and 1973, the NSCT would organize dozens of nonviolent protests, which were intended to call out the Thai government's corruption, the American military occupation, and the mistreatment of civilians. Following a truly successful campaign against corrupt Japanese businesses, the student movement gained over 100,000 members and the confidence necessary to tackle the task of overthrowing their own government. The military rule did not prevent the students from protesting so long as it was nonviolent, and the king of Thailand actually encouraged them.

By the fall of 1973, the movement had gathered nearly half a million supporters. Throughout the months preceding the October revolution, the National Student Center of Thailand secretly created a new constitution and attempted to gather signatures from government officials and public figures who opposed the military rule. However, throughout the end of September and the beginning of October, the police began arresting protestors and became overall more aggressive against the supporters of the movement. All of this tension culminated on October 14th, 1973.

On October 14th, 1973, the student-led protesters flooded the streets and surrounded the royal palace, seeking to speak with the king to request he disband the military rule. Even though the protest began at around sunrise, the October 14th protest gathered more people than ever before, and this larger group meant that the police would not be able to easily disband or arrest all the protestors. To attempt to disperse the large group of protestors, the police released tear gas and became even more aggressive toward the group than they ever had before. This violence was met by rioting from the students, which the police responded to by bringing in armored cars, tanks, helicopters, and military troops. Machine guns were fired from every angle, with the crowd chaotically dispersing, trying to find cover. Many of the surrounding buildings were occupied by government officials, though, and other shelters, such as police booths, had been set on fire by the rioters. Finally, after more than half a day of protesting and rioting, the king stepped in to prevent further bloodshed and declared that Thanom Kittikachorn and Praphas Charusathian had resigned and fled the country. Only after the protest came to an end would the full gravity of the brutal fighting be known. The violence of October 14th, 1973, killed at least seventy-seven people and wounded hundreds. It is estimated at least 800 people were seriously injured.

A Brief Period of Democracy Following the 1973 Thai Popular Uprising

Seeing as King Bhumibol (Rama IX) had gained more influence throughout Sarit Thanarat's and his predecessors' dictatorships, he would be the one to call to an end to the fighting during the brutal 1973 revolution. He also appointed the new prime minister, Dr. Sanya Dharmasakti (or Thammasak), who was a former chief justice, a close advisor to the king, and the former dean of Thammasat University. In a speech made by Dr. Sanya Dharmasakti after being appointed as the interim prime minister of Thailand, he declared that he would draw up a new constitution, form a new government, and move the country toward democracy as quickly as possible. The National Student Center of Thailand (NSCT), who had helped overthrow Sanya Dharmasakti's predecessors, would aid in the creation of the new constitution and would help prevent counterprotests and violence against the nation's new democratic leader. The NSCT's hard work would be appreciated by the government and monarchy until they disbanded exactly a month after the revolutionary protest of October 14th, 1973. Sanya Dharmasakti's new democratic constitution was enacted in 1974, and under his leadership, the country had another brief period free from autocratic government. Although Thanom Kittikachorn was forced to flee

Thailand following the events of the 1973 Thai popular uprising, he kept his position as supreme commander of the armed forces, which he operated from abroad, allowing him to retain significant power within the country.

Return to Military Government

Although Thailand was finally free of the military dictatorship that had been in control of the country for over a quarter of the decade, the nation was, once again, far from peaceful. Following the separation of the National Student Center of Thailand (NSCT) in 1973, the left-winged, democratic students split up into smaller student groups that became gradually more radical throughout the years following the Thai popular uprising. Public opinion of their radical leftist beliefs was not aided by the fact that the government could not triumph over the growing communist governments in neighboring countries, specifically in Vietnam, Cambodia, and Laos. Sanya Dharmasakti's government was unstable, and the population was growing fearful of the potential spread of communism throughout Thailand.

While the fascist military government had stripped the population of many of their rights, they at least had the military prowess to fight the growing communist threats from within and outside the country. The working- and middle-class civilians began forming anti-communist groups to protest the leftist government and to rival the democratic-verging-on-communist student groups. The population, even those who were left-leaning, felt that Thailand required a government that would be stronger than the growing communist threats, and they became dissatisfied with the government's unstable democratic rule. The population's discontent grew and culminated in the bloody and violent 6 October 1976 massacre between the two opposing groups. While the population's discontent grew, Thanom Kittikachorn returned to Thailand. Despite his aggressive policies only years before, upon his return, he was appreciated and celebrated by the royal family and much of the country's population. In 1976, with the support of King Rama IX and the unhappy middle- and working-class civilians, the military overthrew the democratic government and reinstated authoritarian rule. Although it would be Thanom Kittikachorn's return to Thailand that would lead to another coup, he did not directly participate in the new military government.

Considering the end of democracy would bring about another fascist military rule, those who did not agree with the change of government were forced underground. Many of the radical left-leaning students and civilians who had opposed the military government and had helped to take down the military rule during Thanom Kittikachorn's dictatorship would go into hiding in the country's jungles. The population's original unrest toward these radical leftist student groups was not unfounded since many of the extreme students would go on to join communist groups, namely the People's Liberation Army of Thailand (PLAT), which would later become known as the Communist Party of Thailand.

The new military government, led by Thanin Kraivichien, was quick to reinstate the extreme authoritarian practices that the country had gotten used to in the decades before. Almost immediately after taking power, Thanin Kraivichien and his military government abolished Sanya Dharmasakti's democratic constitution and dissolved the parliament. Although the military government had placed Thanin Kraivichien in the role of prime minister to replace the previous democratic government, he very quickly became extreme in a way that even the military government knew would not be accepted, especially so quickly after replacing democracy. With the increased threat from the Communist Party of Thailand and with Thanin Kraivichien's government only focusing on external military affairs, the population was once again growing dissatisfied with the country's leadership. In 1977, the military government led another coup against their own leader, who was replaced with the less extreme General Kriangsak Chomanan.

A Democratic Shift in the Military Government

Although Thanin Kraivichien had been appointed as the prime minister by the authoritarian military government, his staunch right-wing military and political views were too extreme even for the military. He was replaced with Kriangsak Chomanan, who was on the complete opposite end of the spectrum. In the end, he would prove to be too democratic for the military. Kriangsak Chomanan helped establish some democratic practices within the government, including sharing the decision-making process with a parliament, a practice that had been terminated by his predecessor. Under Kriangsak Chomanan, the government enlisted more civilians in official positions, which would, in turn, give some power back to the people of Thailand. He also granted pardons to the radical left-wing revolutionary students, who had been jailed due to their extreme views in the 1976 massacre and when Thanin Kraivichien took over the country. Kriangsak Chomanan would quickly roll out a new, more democratic constitution, and he claimed that he planned to give more power to the parliament in later years. Kriangsak Chomanan's time in office marked a strange time in the country. During his term, the war against communism in the surrounding countries would continue to rage on, leaving many refugees of war trying to enter Thailand's borders. This would force him to adjust the country's strict immigration policies to accept the incoming refugees, who mostly came from Cambodia. Although his time as the leader of Thailand was short-lived, he would achieve many important democratic reforms that would help steer the country toward a less aggressive authoritarian rule in the coming years. By 1979, the military had become increasingly dissatisfied with Kriangsak Chomanan's democratic-leaning practices. Unlike the previous prime ministers, who almost all had resigned due to public resentment following a coup, Kriangsak Chomanan resigned voluntarily. Upon his resignation in 1980, the position of prime minister would be filled by Prem Tinsulanonda.

Prem Tinsulanonda is most notably remembered for eliminating the communist threats within Thailand. Although the Cold War was still raging on during his time as prime minister, the population of Thailand and other foreign countries were beginning to believe that the extreme anti-communist beliefs of Thailand's previous prime ministers were outdated. General Prem Tinsulanonda negotiated with the Communist Party of Thailand and granted amnesty to all Thai insurgents, many of whom had joined the communist movement when they were only young university students. With Prem Tinsulanonda as prime minister, Thailand's economic situation vastly improved. However, despite his improvements to the community, he was still more autocratic and military-driven and less democratic than his predecessor. Throughout his time in office, many rebellions and coups were launched against Prem Tinsulanonda and his military government, and the opposition would even go so far as to attempt to assassinate him. Aware of the public's resent toward him, Prem Tinsulanonda would hold a general election in 1988. He would subsequently be replaced as prime minister by Chatichai Choonhavan, who had won the greatest number of votes that election, making him the first elected government head since the reestablishment of the military government.

The Business Era

Chatichai Choonhavan, the leader of the Chart Thai Party (Thai Nation Party), would be elected prime minister of Thailand, who would help establish an unstable parliamentary rule rather than a military rule in Thailand. Chatichai Choonhavan sought to improve not just Thailand's financial situation but also the economy of Southeast Asia as a whole. Following the communist wars that had plagued the region for years, Chatichai Choonhavan claimed he wanted to transform Indochina from a battlefield into a marketplace. Chatichai filled his government with rich businessmen, and although he helped to improve the nation's and region's economic situation, his practices were extremely corrupt. After it was revealed that political positions were being illegally bought and sold, Chatichai Choonhavan was overthrown in a coup by the National Peacekeeping Council in 1991.

The coup was led by General Sunthorn Kongsompong and Commander in Chief Suchinda Kraprayoon, and although the former would have a larger role in overthrowing Chatichai Choonhavan's government, the latter would end up as the figurehead of the movement. Although Chatichai Choonhavan was not respected once his government's true corrupt practices were revealed, he was at least democratically elected by the people. The overthrowing of his government worried the population, as they did not want to lose their democratic privileges once again. To placate the civilians, the National Peacekeeping Council junta assured the population that proper elections would be held and that the respectable businessman Anand Panyarachun would be appointed as the interim prime minister. Although Anand Panyarachun was appointed by the military-run National Peacekeeping Council, he did not align with them politically and openly disagreed with their practices.

Thailand's Black (or Bloody) May

During the 1992 general election in Thailand, Narong Wongwan from the Justice Unity Party was elected as the new prime minister. However, he never truly assumed the post since he was involved in a scandal not long after being elected. The position of prime minister was instead given to General Suchinda Kraprayoon, who was one of the primary members of the junta that overthrew the Chatichai Choonhavan government. General Suchinda Kraprayoon assumed the position, despite the fact that he had assured the population that he would not become nor run for prime minister following his extreme coup d'état only years before.

The population was not pleased with this change, seeing as they had not chosen General Suchinda Kraprayoon and also due to his promises that he wouldn't assume the leadership position. His ascension in office was met with discontentment from the middle and working classes. Led by Chamlong Srimuang, they formed resistance movements and demonstrated their dissatisfaction with many large-scale protests.

The country was once again divided, this time into those, mainly the military and government, who supported Suchinda Kraprayoon and those led by Chamlong Srimuang, mostly the civilians, who wanted to finally achieve a stable democracy in the country. Unlike the previous revolutions, the democratic movement was not led by students but by a Thai politician and ex-army general. The population's unrest would culminate in May of 1992, which would come to be known as Thailand's Bloody May or Black May. Chamlong Srimuang led over 200,000 protestors to demonstrate in Bangkok, where they were met with resistance and violence from the pro-Suchinda Kraprayoon military. Although the battle only lasted for three days, between May 17th and May 20th, 1992, it is regarded as one of the bleakest periods in Thailand's modern history. Similar to Thailand's popular uprising of 1973, the violence of Bloody May only came to an end when King Bhumibol (Rama IX) intervened. King Bhumibol summoned both the democratic Chamlong Srimuang and the right-wing Suchinda Kraprayoon and delivered a famous discourse to the two men. In the translated words of King Bhumibol: "The nation belongs to everyone, not one or two specific people. Those who confront each other will all be the losers. And the loser of the losers will be the nation...For what purpose are you telling yourself that you're the winner when you're standing upon the ruins and debris?" Only after the king summoned both rivaling leaders could the country account for the damages done during the three days of violence. Bloody May would lead to thousands of arrests, hundreds of wounded civilians, and hundreds of unexplained disappearances. Although there were less than one hundred officially reported deaths, many believe that there were hundreds of more deaths that were hidden from the public eye or never reported upon. Losing almost all public support following the violence in the country's capital,

Suchinda Kraprayoon resigned as prime minister, and Anand Panyarachun was reappointed as interim prime minister by the king until Thailand could hold proper elections.

The Most Democratic Government to Date

Democratic Government

The period following Thailand's Black May in 1992 would be the nation's most democratic period to date. The few months Anand Panyarachun spent as prime minister brought many democratic changes for the population, leading up to a democratic election in September of that year. In contrast with many other foreign countries, which only have two or perhaps three major parties, in Thailand's September 1992 election, there were five parties out of the eligible twelve parties that would amass competitive vote counts. With the votes spread between these five parties, no party would gain an absolute majority in this election or the subsequent elections held in 1995 and 1996. That being said, the Democrat Party, which was founded in 1946 by Khuang Aphaiwong, would head the government throughout the next decade due to its successful coalitions.

In 1992, Thailand's Democrat Party was headed by Chuan Leekpai, a former lawyer who had joined the Democrat Party and became a member of parliament in 1969. By 1991, Chuan Leekpai had risen in the party's ranks, and in 1992, when the Democrat Party took hold of the government, Chuan Leekpai became the country's prime minister. The newly elected prime minister would immediately begin making democratic social reforms, including making strides toward women's equality and lowering the voting age to eighteen to allow a wider margin of the population to elect future politicians. He also established an administrative court and enlarged the House of Representatives.

Despite Chuan Leekpai's rapid political and social democratic reforms, he was extremely slow in making any economic reforms. Although he had the support of the democratic left-leaning population, his approach to Thailand's finances left a good portion of the population dissatisfied. Although the divide had been gradually growing for years, it was during Chuan Leekpai's time in office that Thailand's civilians would truly be split between leftist democratic and right-leaning conservative political beliefs. Bangkok and the nation's southern towns and big cities would find themselves dominated by the more democratic population, while those in the northeast and central plains of the country tended to lean more toward conservative pro-military beliefs.

As Thailand's financial situation continued to worsen, public opinion of Chuan Leekpai, especially from the more conservative Thais, worsened as well. Thailand held another general election in 1995, and this time, Chuan Leekpai did not come out on top. That being said, Chuan Leekpai would be reelected in 1997.

Banharn Silpa-archa and Chavalit Yongchaiyudh, respectively, were the country's prime ministers between Chuan Leekpai's bookend periods in office. The former's time as prime minister was short-lived due to corruption scandals, and the latter would inherit one of the nation's worst economic periods to date. During 1997, while Chavalit Yongchaiyudh was serving as prime minister, Thailand's currency, the baht, was severely depreciated in comparison to the United States dollar at the time. The devaluing of the baht would essentially cause the Asian financial crisis, which would completely ruin Thailand and other Southeast Asian countries' economies in the subsequent years. Before the end of 1997, the Thai stock market would completely drop, and the nation would acquire severe debt due to necessary financial help from the International Monetary Fund (IMF), which would only aid to cripple their economy over the following years. Although many people associate the country's economic crisis with Chuan Leekpai's poor economic practices in the years preceding the Asian financial crisis, Chavalit Yongchaiyudh would take the brunt of the blame and would resign in late 1997. The country held an election once again in 1997, and Chuan Leekpai was once more elected as prime minister. During Chuan Leekpai's second term, the government was unstable, just as the two democratic governments run by his predecessors had been. Although Chuan Leekpai's government would enact a new constitution that would allow the population the most democratic freedoms they had ever seen, with the constitution having been completed during Chavalit Yongchaiyudh's time in office, Chuan Leekpai did little to aid the struggling economy. Chuan Leekpai would hold his position as prime minister until the country's election in 2001.

The Thaksin Era

Chuan Leekpai was succeeded by Thaksin Shinawatra, who was the founder of the Thai Rak Thai ("Thais Love Thais") Party. Thaksin Shinawatra had originally trained to be a police officer and even earned a scholarship to study criminal justice in the United States to advance his career. Over the years subsequent to earning his degrees, Thaksin Shinawatra rose in the ranks of the police force and spent much of his spare time focusing on computer technology, which he was extremely gifted in. Unfortunately, he could not find employment in the field, seeing as it was the 1980s. Toward the end of the 1980s, Thaksin Shinawatra would leave the force and begin investing time and money into his technological businesses, joined by his wife, Potjaman. The road was not easy for the pair, but by the end of the decade, Thaksin Shinawatra's dedication paid off, as he would found a mobile phone operator and a telecommunications company, which would, by the 1990s, make him one of the wealthiest people in Thailand.

Thaksin Shinawatra had brushed with politics throughout his career, but it was not until 1994 that he would take a vested interest in becoming a member of the political sphere. In 1998, he founded the Thai Rak Thai (TRT) Party, which would be elected as the governing party in the 2001 election. Thaksin Shinawatra would officially succeed Chuan Leekpai as prime minister in February of that year. In many ways, Thaksin became the politician that much of the population had been waiting for, seeing as he understood the economy, believed in democracy, and aligned politically with the views of the more conservative population in northern and northeastern Thailand. With his impressive business record, he was also supported by Thailand's elite business owners.

When Thaksin and his party assumed office at the beginning of 2001, he almost immediately set out on delivering the promises that he had made during his campaign. The rapid reforms were a welcome change, seeing as how his predecessors were criticized for their ineffective, slow output speed. Thaksin increased his popularity with the rural population, as he commenced rural development and set forth agrarian debt relief. During his time as prime minister, Thaksin Shinawatra set up a more affordable and accessible healthcare system to help the lower-income population in Thailand and invested and reformed the education system. Thaksin was largely respected due to his swift actions throughout his entire time in office. This was not just limited to delivering on his campaign promises but also in his response to the 2004 Indian Ocean tsunami.

Despite all of Thaksin's positive reforms made throughout his time as prime minister, his private business practices made him somewhat of a controversial leader. Before he was elected as prime minister, Thaksin Shinawatra and his Thai Rak Thai Party funded campaigns and advertising with private funds, much of which came from his own financial resources. Seeing as this had not yet been done before, many people saw this practice as buying votes. Throughout his term, he would face many prosecutions on different accounts relating to his secretive financial and business practices. Although he would be reelected in the subsequent election, and although he was extremely popular and highly praised, Thaksin's time in office was marked by the incredible scrutiny relating to his potential fraud, corruption, and cronyism.

An election was held in 2005, and for the first time in Thailand's history, Thaksin Shinawatra and his Thai Rak Thai Party won by an absolute majority, which would give the party a majority of the seats in parliament and give Thaksin ultimately more control than his democratic predecessors had. However, before a year had passed, Thaksin would become increasingly controversial. He would sell his self-founded telecommunications company in early 2006, but he was secretive about the taxes involved in the selling process. On top of that, Thaksin Shinawatra had begun taking advantage of King Bhumibol's old age in an attempt to gain more power before the king's successor took over. To add fuel to the fire, in his later years, Thaksin Shinawatra was addressing foreign insurgencies with military force rather than political solutions. Overall, the population became dissatisfied with their once beloved leader, as it seemed he was attempting to manipulate the royal family, the parliament, and the population.

Toward the end of 2005, the population's resentment was growing, which they demonstrated through rallies staged in the nation's capital. The resistance movement, which was run by the urban middle class, became known officially as the People's Alliance for Democracy (PAD) and unofficially as the Yellow Shirts since, as the name would suggest, they wore yellow shirts at their rallies. Although Thaksin was aware of the growing urban dissatisfaction, he was still confident in the rural population's support, and at the beginning of 2006, he called for an election to prove his popularity. While his party did win by a majority, the election had been boycotted, and the results were ruled invalid. Although Thaksin remained as interim prime minister throughout the year, by the fall, he was overthrown by a military coup led by Sonthi Boonyaratglin, who would assume leadership until being replaced by Surayud Chulanont. Thaksin Shinawatra would be exiled from the country, and his finances would continue to be investigated. In 2008, Thaksin was prosecuted and served time on the grounds of corruption.

Surayud Chulanont would hold the leadership position until the country would hold its first election following the coup of Thaksin Shinawatra in 2008. Samak Sundaravej, who helped to form his pro-Thaksin People Power Party (PPP), was elected as prime minister in the 2008 election. Considering his support of the ousted prime minister, many believed Samak Sundaravej and his government were controlled by Thaksin Shinawatra behind the scenes, although these claims were never proven to be true. However, regardless of Thaksin Shinawatra's involvement in the government or not, the urban middle-class population who had protested Thaksin's leadership were not pleased with their new government.

Protests by Both the Yellow Shirts and Red Shirts

Considering the fact that the newly elected People Power Party was completely pro-Thaksin, political unrest continued to grow. The Yellow Shirts (People's Alliance for Democracy, or PAD), which was an ever-growing democratic, Thaksin resistance group, continued to stage protests following Samak Sundaravej's election as prime minister. They felt that no change had been made from their last protest that had helped to overthrow Thaksin since Samak Sundaravej was essentially no different than his predecessor. They believed that Samak was merely standing in until the government could get Thaksin back in office. In September of 2008, Samak Sundaravej, who was forced to resign due to illegally accepting payments for TV cooking show appearances, was succeeded by Somchai Wongsawat, who was actually Thaksin's brother-in-law.

The election of Thaksin's brother-in-law, Somchai Wongsawat, unsurprisingly caused significant political unrest in the country, especially those in the Yellow Shirts (PAD) movement. To oppose the growing anti-Thaksin Yellow Shirts movement, those who had remained supporters of Thaksin formed a rival movement called the United Front for Democracy Against Dictatorship (UDD), which, somewhat similar to their opposition, became known as the Red Shirts due to the color of their uniform. Many of the Red Shirts lived in rural northern and northeastern Thailand, although there were some urban supporters of the movement as well.

Over the subsequent years, the two groups clashed many times, with the yellow-shirted PAD members protesting in hopes of electing a new anti-Thaksin government and the red-shirted UDD supporting Thaksin and his successors' governments. In 2008, the anti-Thaksin PAD flooded the Bangkok airports with protestors, which grew to become violent quite quickly. Only a few months later, on December 2nd, 2008, Somchai Wongsawat was forcibly removed from office and replaced by the Democrat Party's leader, Abhisit Vejjajiva. Meanwhile, the red-shirted UDD organized their own protests, which became significantly more frequent and aggressive following the removal of Somchai Wongsawat.

The Red Shirts' protesting would culminate at the beginning of 2010 following Thaksin's guilty charges of corruption during his time as prime minister. The pro-Thaksin movement protested both the government's order to seize Thaksin's fortune and Somchai Wongsawat's replacement, who they demanded should resign. In March of that year, the Red Shirts flooded Bangkok's commercial district, where they protested for two months. Although the first month of protesting was mostly nonviolent, by mid-April, the government became more aggressive toward the Red Shirts' occupation of the city's shopping district. As a result, the second month of protesting became increasingly more violent until May, when the military finally used force to remove the protestors. This would end in a bloody battle on May 19th, with shopping centers being set on fire, hundreds of protestors being arrested and/or injured, and almost 100 people being killed.

These protests would not bring the Red Shirts any real success until July of 2011, when the pro-Thaksin Phak Puea Thai Party (PPT) was elected, with Thaksin's younger sister, Yingluck Shinawatra, as its head. Although Yingluck Shinawatra would become Thailand's first female prime minister, she was a wildly controversial leader. Her election would be met with political unrest from those in the People's Alliance for Democracy (the Yellow Shirts movement), who believed she was only a proxy for her brother. At the beginning of her term, she swiftly aided those who had been affected by the country's heavy monsoon rains, but her positive public opinion was short-lived. First, Yingluck Shinawatra was involved in a scandal surrounding corrupt rice sales, which ended up greatly crippling Thailand's economy, and then her government attempted to introduce an amnesty bill. This bill would have granted amnesty to all the politicians involved in the previous years' political drama, including Thaksin. This was, of course, met with political protests from the Yellow Shirts. Shortly after attempting to pass the amnesty bill, Yingluck Shinawatra would be forced to resign, and her position would be filled once again by an interim prime minister.

The End of Democracy and the Beginning of a New Military Dictatorship

Yingluck Shinawatra's interim successor, Niwattumrong Boonsongpaisan, was in office for around two weeks before the government was overthrown once again by another military coup in 2014, this time led by the highest-ranking member of the Thai military, General Prayuth Chan-ocha (or Prayut Chan-o-cha). In May of 2014, General Prayuth Chan-ocha assumed the position as the nation's prime minister, a position he still holds today at the beginning of 2021. General Prayuth Chan-ocha would immediately invoke military law, and although it was certainly not the first time the population of Thailand had endured an authoritarian military dictatorship, the shift of power was incredibly difficult, as the nation had become quite used to democracy.

Prayuth Chan-ocha's military government sought to establish stability in the country that had faced so many struggles for power in the years since the fall of the monarchy; thus, his government became known as the National Council for Peace and Order (NCPO). In the year following the 2014 coup, Prayuth Chan-ocha stripped the population of many of their democratic rights under martial law. He quickly imposed a curfew, limited public gatherings, banned media that spoke out against his government, and took away the right to protest for both the Red Shirt and Yellow Shirt movements. On April 1st, 2015, just under a year after assuming the leadership of the country, Prayuth Chan-ocha lifted martial law and created a constitution, which underwent many alterations over the next few months until finally being released in August of 2016. On October 13th, 2016, King Bhumibol (King Rama IX), the monarch who had brought the spotlight and influence back to Thailand's royal family, passed away at eighty-eight years old. He was succeeded by his son Vajiralongkorn, who would become known as King Rama X, the country's tenth king in an unbroken familial chain of monarchs known as the Chakri dynasty. King Vajiralongkorn is associated with many controversies; their full extent is unknown, as after ascending the throne, Prayuth Chan-ocha enacted strict lèse-majesté laws, which prevents anyone from speaking ill of the king within or outside of the country. These lèse-majesté laws are just another example of Prayuth Chan-ocha's strict authoritarian rule, which upset both the population of Thailand and the foreign countries with whom Thailand once held strong alliances. In response to foreign pressure, Prayuth Chan-ocha promised the country would hold an election in 2017, and although this would be delayed, Thailand would have its first election since being placed under martial rule in 2019. Prayuth Chan-ocha was reelected as prime minister, and his government still remains in power as of January 2021.

Conclusion

As of January 2021, Thailand is still led by a military government, which may come as a surprise to those who did not have a full grasp of the tumultuous political history of the country. Between the years 1238 and 1932, the country was led by an absolute monarchy. During the Sukhothai, Ayutthaya, and Thonburi periods, the kings would help to forge much of the nation's unique culture through establishing its traditions, religion, and language. In 1782, King Rama I, the first member of the still-ruling Chakri dynasty, would take the throne and move the capital city to Bangkok. Between 1782 and 1932, the country, which was controlled by Rama I and his relatives, would establish its global presence and modernize many of its practices, beliefs, and traditions into what they are today. Though Thailand, then known as Siam, spent its entire history until the 20th century under an absolute monarchist rule, foreign countries were developing their own governments, which were separate from the ruling crown. It would be Western-educated Thai students, who had begun their plotting in Europe, who would overthrow and finally put an end to the absolute monarchy through the Thai revolution of 1932.

Following the Thai revolution of 1932, the government was almost never stable, as it constantly shifted between democratic and authoritarian military governments. The curious thing was that every time the democrats would take office, Thailand would need a stricter government to carry them through economic challenges or military threats, and every time the military government took office, they would help solve those issues but take their autocratic rule too far, stripping the population of their rights, which would end in protests and revolutions. For the past six years, the government has returned to a military dictatorship. However, who knows how long it will last, as the country has never been able to strike a balance between the two radical forms of government.

Here's another book by Captivating History that you might like

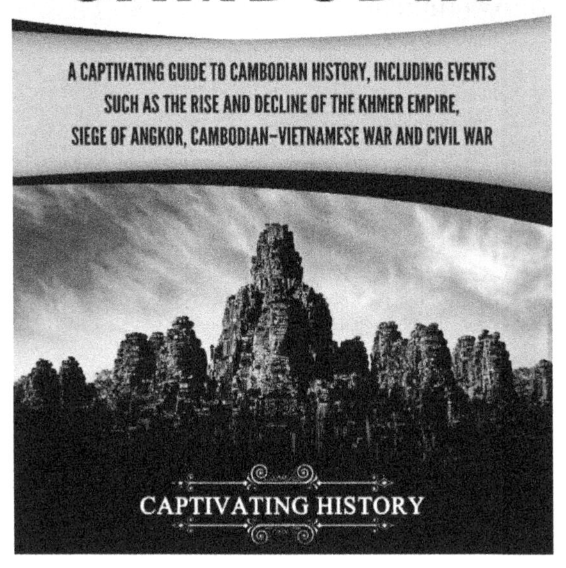

Free Bonus from Captivating History (Available for a Limited time)

Hi History Lovers!

Now you have a chance to join our exclusive history list so you can get your first history ebook for free as well as discounts and a potential to get more history books for free! Simply visit the link below to join.

Captivatinghistory.com/ebook

Also, make sure to follow us on Facebook, Twitter and Youtube by searching for Captivating History.

Bibliography

Ancient Origins. "Kingdom of Sukhothai and the Birth of Thailand." Ancient Origins. April 17, 2020. Accessed December 2020. https://www.ancient-origins.net/ancient-places-asia/sukhothai-kingdom-0013580.

Anto, Meiri. "Thai Students Overthrow Military Thanom Regime, 1973." Global Nonviolent

Action Database. May 13, 2013. Accessed January 2021.

https://nvdatabase.swarthmore.edu/content/thai-students-overthrow-military-thanom-regime-1973.

Asia Highlights. "Sukhothai Kingdom." Asia Highlights. May 28, 2020. Accessed December 2020. https://www.asiahighlights.com/thailand/sukhothai-kingdom.

Asiaweek. "Newsmakers." *Asiaweek*, July 30, 2000.

https://web.archive.org/web/20060322141459/http://www.pathfinder.com/asiaweek/magazine/2000/0630/newsmakers.html.

BBC. "Kneeling before a King: The Moment That Shook a Nation." *BBC*, October 13, 2016. Accessed January 2021. https://www.bbc.com/news/world-asia-37650466.

BBC. "Thailand Profile - Timeline." BBC News. March 7, 2019. Accessed December 2020. https://www.bbc.com/news/world-asia-15641745.

Bentley, R. Alexander, Michael Pietrusewsky, Michele T. Douglas, and Tim C. Atkinson. "Matrilocality during the Prehistoric Transition to Agriculture in Thailand?: Antiquity." Cambridge Core. March 10, 2015. Accessed December 2020.

https://www.cambridge.org/core/journals/antiquity/article/matrilocality-during-the-prehistoric-transition-to-agriculture-in-thailand/641E2C761F097C80C13C153698AE9599.

Britannica, T. Editors of Encyclopedia. "Khmer." Encyclopedia Britannica. April 18, 2020. Accessed December 2020. https://www.britannica.com/topic/Khmer.

Britannica, The Editors of Encyclopedia. "Sukhothai Kingdom." Encyclopedia Britannica. April 10, 2009. Accessed December 2020. https://www.britannica.com/place/Sukhothai-kingdom.

Britannica, The Editors of Encyclopedia. "Lan Na." Encyclopedia Britannica. April 02, 2009. Accessed December 2020. https://www.britannica.com/place/Lan-Na.

Britannica, The Editors of Encyclopedia. "Tai." Encyclopedia Britannica. July 7, 2011. Accessed December 2020. https://www.britannica.com/topic/Tai-people.

Britannica, The Editors of Encyclopedia. "Ayutthaya." Encyclopedia Britannica. August 18, 2015. Accessed December 2020. https://www.britannica.com/place/Ayutthaya-Thailand.

Britannica, The Editors of Encyclopedia. "Toungoo Dynasty." Encyclopedia Britannica. August 8, 2017. Accessed December 2020. https://www.britannica.com/topic/Toungoo-dynasty.

Britannica, The Editors of Encyclopedia. "Chakkri Dynasty." Encyclopedia Britannica. April 26, 2017. Accessed December 2020. https://www.britannica.com/topic/Chakkri-dynasty.

Britannica, The Editors of Encyclopedia. "Dvaravati." Encyclopedia Britannica. May 29, 2018. Accessed December 2020. https://www.britannica.com/place/Dvaravati.

Britannica, The Editors of Encyclopedia. "Baht." Encyclopedia Britannica. September 23, 2019. Accessed January 2021. https://www.britannica.com/topic/baht.

Britannica, The Editors of Encyclopedia. "Mon." Encyclopedia Britannica. April 18, 2020. Accessed December 2020. https://www.britannica.com/topic/Mon-people.

Britannica, The Editors of Encyclopedia. "Ramkhamhaeng." Encyclopedia Britannica. December 2020. Accessed December 2020. https://www.britannica.com/biography/Ramkhamhaeng.

Britannica, The Editors of Encyclopedia. "Naresuan." Encyclopedia Britannica. December 2020. Accessed December 2020. https://www.britannica.com/biography/Naresuan.

Britannica, The Editors of Encyclopedia. "Trailok." Encyclopedia Britannica. December 1, 2020. Accessed December 2020. https://www.britannica.com/biography/Trailok.

Britannica, The Editors of Encyclopedia. "Hsinbyushin." Encyclopedia Britannica. 2020. Accessed December 2020. https://www.britannica.com/biography/Hsinbyushin.

Britannica, The Editors of Encyclopedia. "Taksin." Encyclopedia Britannica. April 13, 2020. Accessed December 2020. https://www.britannica.com/biography/Taksin.

Britannica, The Editors of Encyclopedia. "Rama I." Encyclopedia Britannica. September 3, 2020. Accessed December 2020. https://www.britannica.com/biography/Rama-I.

Britannica, The Editors of Encyclopedia. "Rama II." Encyclopedia Britannica. July 17, 2020. Accessed December 2020. https://www.britannica.com/biography/Rama-II.

Britannica, The Editors of Encyclopedia. "Rama III." Encyclopedia Britannica. March 29, 2020. Accessed December 2020. https://www.britannica.com/biography/Rama-III.

Britannica, The Editors of Encyclopedia. "Mongkut." Encyclopedia Britannica. October 14, 2020. Accessed December 2020. https://www.britannica.com/biography/Mongkut.

Britannica, The Editors of Encyclopedia. "Chulalongkorn." Encyclopedia Britannica. October 19, 2020. Accessed December 2020. https://www.britannica.com/biography/Chulalongkorn.

Britannica, The Editors of Encyclopedia. "Somdet Chao Phraya Si Suriyawong." Encyclopedia Britannica. December 2020. Accessed December 2020.

https://www.britannica.com/biography/Somdet-Chao-Phraya-Si-Suriyawong.

Britannica, The Editors of Encyclopedia. "Vajiravudh." Encyclopedia Britannica. 2020. Accessed December 2020. https://www.britannica.com/biography/Vajiravudh.

Britannica, The Editors of Encyclopedia. "Prajadhipok." Encyclopedia Britannica. November 4, 2020. Accessed December 2020. https://www.britannica.com/biography/Prajadhipok.

Britannica, The Editors of Encyclopedia. "Pridi Phanomyong." Encyclopedia Britannica. May 7, 2020. Accessed December 2020. https://www.britannica.com/biography/Pridi-Phanomyong.

Britannica, The Editors of Encyclopedia. "Luang Phibunsongkhram." Encyclopedia Britannica. July 10, 2020. Accessed December 2020. https://www.britannica.com/biography/Luang-Phibunsongkhram.

Britannica, The Editors of Encyclopedia. "Ananda Mahidol." Encyclopedia Britannica.

September 16, 2020. Accessed January 2021. https://www.britannica.com/biography/Ananda-Mahidol.

Britannica, The Editors of Encyclopedia. "Sarit Thanarat." Encyclopedia Britannica. December 4, 2020. Accessed January 2021. https://www.britannica.com/biography/Sarit-Thanarat.

Britannica, The Editors of Encyclopedia. "Thanom Kittikachorn." Encyclopedia Britannica. August 7, 2020. Accessed January 2021. https://www.britannica.com/biography/Thanom-Kittikachorn.

Britannica, The Editors of Encyclopedia. "Chuan Leekpai." Encyclopedia Britannica. July 24, 2020. Accessed January 2021. https://www.britannica.com/biography/Chuan-Leekpai.

Britannica, The Editors of Encyclopedia. "Thaksin Shinawatra." Encyclopedia Britannica. July 22, 2020. Accessed January 2021. https://www.britannica.com/biography/Thaksin-Shinawatra.

Chemical Engineering Kmutt. "KING RAMA III [Nang Klao] 1824 - 1851." Arts Kmutt. 2004. Accessed December 2020. http://arts.kmutt.ac.th/lng104/lng104_2003/g5/BIOGRAPHY of King RAMA III.htm.

Court of Justice Thailand. "History of the Court of Justice." Court of Justice Thailand. 2020. Accessed December 2020. https://www.coj.go.th/th/content/page/index/id/91989.

Devex. "Ministry of Interior (Thailand)." Devex. 2021. Accessed January 2021. https://www.devex.com/organizations/ministry-of-interior-thailand-135202.

Erlanger, Steven. "Thailand Seeks to Shape a 'Golden Peninsula'." *The New York Times*, April 30, 1989. Accessed January 2021. https://www.nytimes.com/1989/04/30/world/thailand-seeks-to-shape-a-golden-peninsula.html.

Google Arts & Culture. "Rama III." Google. 2020. Accessed December 2020.

https://artsandculture.google.com/entity/rama-iii/m01cy0z?hl=en.

Government of Singapore. "Bowring Treaty Signed with Bangkok." History SG. August 1, 2019. Accessed January 2021.

https://eresources.nlb.gov.sg/history/events/ae996879-bb92-4dab-a62b-594824b803e6.

Hafner, J. A., Keyes, Charles F. Keyes, and Jane E. "Thailand." Encyclopedia Britannica. January 24, 2021. Accessed December 2020. https://www.britannica.com/place/Thailand.

Hamilton, Elizabeth. "Bronze from Ban Chiang, Thailand: A View from the Laboratory."

Expedition Magazine Bronze from Ban Chiang Thailand A View from the Laboratory

Comments. July 15, 2001. Accessed December 2020.

https://www.penn.museum/sites/expedition/bronze-from-ban-chiang-thailand/.

Hays, Jeffrey. "Ancient History of Thailand, Origin of the Thais and the Thai Name and World's First Bronze Age Culture." Facts and Details. May 2014. Accessed December 2020. http://factsanddetails.com/southeast-asia/Thailand/sub5_8a/entry-3184.html.

Hays, Jeffrey. "Military Rule in Thailand after World War II." Facts and Details. May 2014. Accessed January 2021. http://factsanddetails.com/southeast-asia/Thailand/sub5_8a/entry-3189.html.

Hays, Jeffrey. "Thailand in the 1990s: The 1992 Demonstrations, Short-Lived Leaders and the 1997 Asian Financial Crisis." Facts and Details. May 2014. Accessed January 2021. http://factsanddetails.com/southeast-asia/Thailand/sub5_8a/entry-3193.html.

Hays, Jeffrey. "Sukhothai and Early Thai Kings." Facts and Details. August 2020. Accessed December 2020. http://factsanddetails.com/southeast-asia/Thailand/sub5_8a/entry-3185.html.

Hollar, Sherman. "Samak Sundaravej." Encyclopedia Britannica. November 20, 2020. Accessed January 2021. https://www.britannica.com/biography/Samak-Sundaravej.

Hulme, Kyle. "This Is How Thailand Really Got Its Name." Culture Trip. March 10, 2018. Accessed December 2020. https://theculturetrip.com/asia/thailand/articles/land-of-the-free-how-thailand-got-its-name/.

Insight Guides. Insightguides.com. 2020. Accessed December 2020.

https://www.insightguides.com/destinations/asia-pacific/thailand/historical-highlights.

Institute for Southeast Asian Archaeology. "The Ban Chiang Project." Institute for Southeast Asian Archaeology ISEAA. 2018. Accessed December 2020. https://iseaarchaeology.org/ban-chiang-project/background/.

Institute for Southeast Asian Archaeology. "The Ban Chiang Project – METALS MONOGRAPH." Institute for Southeast Asian Archaeology ISEAA. 2018.

Lim, Eric. "Phibun Songkhram - the Master of the Coup D'état." Tour Bangkok Legacies. 2018. Accessed January 2021. https://www.tour-bangkok-legacies.com/phibun-songkhram.html.

Lim, Eric. "Pridi Banomyong the Father of Thai Democracy." Tour Bangkok Legacies. 2020. Accessed January 2021. https://www.tour-bangkok-legacies.com/pridi-banomyong.html.

Lithai, Frank Reynolds, and Mari B. Reynolds. *Three Worlds According to King Ruang, a Thai Buddhist Cosmology.* Berkeley, CA: Center for South and Southeast Asian Studies, University of California., 1982.

Lonely Planet. "Thailand in Detail." Lonely Planet. August 21, 2019. Accessed December 2020. https://www.lonelyplanet.com/thailand/narratives/background/history.

Mishra, Patit Paban. *The History of Thailand.* Santa Barbara, CA: Greenwood, 2010.

Mudar, Karen M. *Evidence for Prehistoric Dryland Farming in Mainland Southeast Asia: Results of Regional Survey in Lopburi Province, Thailand.* Report. University of Hawai'i Press (Honolulu). 1995.

Muntarbhorn, Vitit. "Lessons of 'Black May' 1992 and the 2006 Coup." *Bangkok Post,* May 23, 2014. Accessed January 2021. https://www.bangkokpost.com/opinion/opinion/411309/lessons-of-black-may-1992-and-the-2006-coup.

Nationsonline.org, Klaus Kästle. "History of Thailand." History of Thailand. 2020. Accessed December 2020. https://www.nationsonline.org/oneworld/History/Thailand-history.htm.

Phattanarat, Siwanit. "Cradle of the Thai Nation: Sukhothai, the Dawn of Happiness." Thailand Guide. January 2003. Accessed December 2020. http://www.thailand-guide.com/benjarong/beyondphuket/sukhothai.htm.

Pike, John. "Thailand - Thonburi Period (1767-1782)." Global Security. August 4, 2012.

Accessed December 2020. https://www.globalsecurity.org/military/world/thailand/history-thonburi.htm.

Plengmaneepun, Suphaphan. "Thisrupt History: How the Cholera Outbreak Came from an Evil Spirit and Became a Name-calling Insult." Thisrupt. March 16, 2020. Accessed December 2020. https://thisrupt.co/society/thisrupt-history-cholera-insult.

Renown Travel. "Sukhothai Kingdom History." History of the Sukhothai Kingdom. 2020. Accessed December 2020. https://www.renown-travel.com/historicalsites/sukhothai/history.html.

Royal Thai Consulate. "Thailand History." Royal Thai Consulate General, Hong Kong. 2020. Accessed December 2020. http://www.thai-consulate.org.hk/webroot/ENG/Thailand/History1.htm.

Smith, Brian K., J.A.B. Van Buitenen, Wendy Doniger, Vasudha Narayanan, Edward C. Dimock, Arthur Llewellyn Basham, and Ann G. Gold. "Hinduism." Encyclopedia Britannica. November 30, 2020. Accessed December 2020. https://www.britannica.com/topic/Hinduism.

Stowe, Judy. "Obituary: Seni Pramoj." *Independent,* July 29, 1997. Accessed January 2021. https://www.independent.co.uk/news/people/obituary-seni-pramoj-1253268.html.

The New York Times. "New Thai Premier Named as Students Battle Troops." *The New York Times,* October 15, 1973. https://www.nytimes.com/1973/10/15/archives/new-thai-premier-named-as-students-battle-troops-student-rioting.html.

The New York Times. "Another Coup in Thailand." *The New York Times,* October 21, 1977. Accessed January 2021. https://www.nytimes.com/1977/10/21/archives/another-coup-in-thailand.html.

The Phra Racha Wang Derm Restoration Foundation. "King Taksin The Great." King Taksin. 2013. Accessed December 2020. http://www.wangdermpalace.org/King Taksin.html.

The Times. "General Kriangsak Chomanan." *The Times,* January 22, 2004. Accessed January 2021. https://www.thetimes.co.uk/article/general-kriangsak-chomanan-jnxhzflxncv.

Tim's Thailand. "About the Ramkhamhaeng Inscription." Tim's Thailand. May 8, 2018. Accessed December 2020. https://www.timsthailand.com/about-ramkhamhaeng-inscription/.

Tourism Authority of Thailand. “The King Taksin Shrine.” The Official Website of Tourism Authority of Thailand. 2020. Accessed December 2020. https://www.tourismthailand.org/Attraction/the-king-taksin-shrine.

TravelOnline. “Thailand Culture & History.” TravelOnline. 2020. Accessed December 2020.
https://www.travelonline.com/thailand/history.

U.S. Embassy & Consulate in Thailand. “Policy & History.” U.S. Embassy & Consulate in

Thailand. November 19, 2019. Accessed January 2021.
https://th.usembassy.gov/our-relationship/policy-history/.

UNESCO World Heritage Centre. “The King Ram Khamhaeng Inscription.” The King Ram Khamhaeng Inscription | United Nations Educational, Scientific and Cultural Organization. 2017. Accessed December 2020.
http://www.unesco.org/new/en/communication-and-information/memory-of-the-world/register/full-list-of-registered-heritage/registered-heritage-page-8/the-king-ram-khamhaeng-inscription/.

UNESCO World Heritage Centre. “Ban Chiang Archaeological Site.” UNESCO World Heritage Centre. 2020. Accessed December 2020. https://whc.unesco.org/en/list/55/.

Vandenberg, Tricky. “History of Ayutthaya - Historical Events - Timeline 1300-1399.”

Ayutthaya History. 2020. Accessed December 2020.
https://www.ayutthaya-history.com/Historical_Events13.html.

Wiener, James Blake. “Sukhothai.” Ancient History Encyclopedia. October 12, 2018. Accessed December 2020.
https://www.ancient.eu/Sukhothai/.

Wyatt, David K. *Thailand: A Short History.* New Haven, CT: Yale University Press, 2004.

สารนิเทศสัมพันธ์ มหาวิทยาลัยรามคำแหง. “The Inscription of King Ramkamhaeng the Great.”

[illegible] ฯ 1. 2020. Accessed December 2020.
http://www.info.ru.ac.th/province/Sukhotai/srjsd11-4en.htm.

Made in United States
North Haven, CT
02 March 2024